The Rich Revolution

BRUCE BISHOP

The Rich Revolution
First published in 2013 by

Filament Publishing Ltd
16 Croydon Road,
Waddon,
Croydon,
Surrey CR0 4PA
United Kingdom
Tel: 020 8688 2598
info@filamentpublishing.com
www.filamentpublishing.com

Design and layout by ALS Designs. www.als-designs.co.uk

Printed by CreateSpace.

ISBN 978-1-908691-90-3

WHY THIS BOOK IS FOR YOU

One of the main reasons I wrote this book is because if I'd known at 21 what I know now, I could have achieved so much more in a FRACTION of the time! That's why I'm now passionate about sharing what I've learned.

I've never been more than an ordinary guy with an ordinary income and yet have now achieved financial freedom by applying some simple common sense to my finances. Nothing complex or too sophisticated. I hope you take these simple strategies that made this possible and use them to create a solid and secure financial future for yourself. Believe me, 'If I can do it, anyone can'.

Along with an ever-increasing number of people, I have completely lost faith in pensions as a way of providing for our retirement. I now think it's high time we woke up and took responsibility for our own futures.

There are some fundamental differences between the rich and the rest of us. By understanding these simple differences and implementing them in YOUR OWN life, you can become rich, which in my eyes means financial independence AND time freedom. And contrary to popular belief you don't have to have an amazing income, change career or start a new business, this can be done from your present career with just an average income… those of you who know me will have heard me say time and time again. "It doesn't matter what you earn, it's what you do with what you earn".

Bruce

FOREWORD FROM RON G HOLLAND

Money makes money and the money, money makes, makes more money!

I love serious, pragmatic books that show you how to make money and accumulate assets, even in a tough economic climate. This is one of those books that you will not only enjoy and read over and over again; but because it is a step-by-step approach to making money, you'll find yourself automatically and rapidly going up the ladder of success and accomplishing all of your goals. All excuses and obstacles are overcome because you will be shown how to start your quest for wealth starting exactly where you are, which may be with little or no resources, even in debt.

This book is an incredible road map that will take you on the most exciting and profitable journey of your life, but will not leave you stranded in the wilderness not knowing what to do next. You will be compelled to take action because the guidelines are so concise you'll be anxious to start your own journey and turn your life around for ever.

Onward and Upward, **Ron G Holland**

Author of *Talk & Grow Rich* and *The Eureka! Enigma* and Founder of *The Apprentice Millionaires Club*

INDEX

Join the RICH REVOLUTION at **www.therichrevolution.com**

"We can have more than we've got because we can become more than we are."

Jim Rohn

CHAPTER 1

An alternative to your pay cheque

This feels really strange – my sitting here about to write a book... You see, I've never been the most academic of people, and although I enjoyed my school years, I never did that well. I'm sure most of my teachers would rather I hadn't been there, and towards the end I often wasn't! So, this isn't going to be the finest piece of literature you have ever read but I hope you will take this information and use it to create a solid and secure financial future for yourself.

What I am going to share with you is how to acquire income-earning assets throughout your working life that will support you for the rest of your days.

Along with an ever-increasing number of people, I have completely lost faith in pensions as a way of providing for retirement. I now think it's high time we woke up and took responsibility for our own futures. I find it quite remarkable that we send our kids to school to be educated for around 15 to 20 years and yet most of them still leave without a clue about how our day-to-day finances work! I'm sure, however, that if we just taught children the basic principles of how money *really* works, the society we live in would actually be a better place. I'm not trying to knock the education system because for the most part it does an amazing job. I just feel that in this day and age, with the knowledge and technology

"The real opportunity for success lies within the person and not in the job."

Zig Ziglar

we have available to us, we should be able to educate our kids how to cope financially throughout their lives a great deal better than we do.

One of the things I talk about later on in this book is how successful people use experts and other people's knowledge. They understand that to learn about and do everything yourself would take up too much valuable time. Therefore they don't spend time and effort doing everything themselves; instead they seek out experts and employ them to undertake the task required. The point about an expert though is that they must be capable of justifying that title. Therefore I feel the need to qualify *myself* as someone who is worthy of talking about securing *your* financial future.

I would like to point out right from the start that I've never been more than an ordinary guy with an ordinary income. It is important for you to understand this as it is from that ordinary income that I was able to retire at the age of 44. I believe the most important part about this book is that you understand that if *I can do it, you can too*. During my working life my main focus was to build a successful and profitable business, and it took me nearly 15 years to realise that what I had achieved in property far outweighed anything I'd achieved in business! So far I've developed over £10 million worth of property and I have a portfolio worth over £4 million – most of which was achieved part-time because until 2005 property was nothing more to me than a hobby! I don't say any of this to blow my own trumpet – it's just to let you know why I believe I'm qualified to talk about you making investments for your future.

From my experience of something I achieved part-time I hope to share with you some really simple and practical advice that will enable you to achieve even more in far less time. I also think it's important to point out that this book is not information on how to become a property investor. It's about laying the foundations to creating wealth and can apply to anyone whatever your present income level is, large or small. You see,

*"A successful man is
one who can lay a firm
foundation with the bricks
others have thrown at him."*

David Brinkley

once you've got the foundations and basic understanding of wealth creation, you can then go on to invest in anything you like, whether it's property, stocks and shares, or whatever type of investment interests you. It's like the analogy of building a house on good foundations or building it on sand. Build it on a good foundation and it will stand strong, whereas build it on sand, it will eventually crack and collapse.

Let me tell you a little bit more about why I believe that *if I can do it, you can too.*

The main reason I failed to do well at school was the fact that I had dyslexia. Back in the seventies and eighties when my teachers were attempting to educate me, dyslexia was virtually unrecognised. I remember how frustrated I used to feel at not being able to read and record information in the way my classmates could. Looking back it was one of the main reasons I became disruptive in class because, if you place someone in a position of constant failure, he will eventually give up and quit. As a person who prides himself on seeing things through to a successful conclusion - as shown by the results I've achieved throughout my working life, I have to admit that my school career is undoubtedly my all-time greatest failure. I still have mostly unpleasant memories of the anger and frustration caused by constantly being made to look stupid and failing in front of my peers, as well as being bullied by teachers into trying to do something I just couldn't do – read. As far as I was concerned, asking me to participate in reading and spelling was like asking someone on crutches to sprint.

In those days, dyslexia wasn't understood; most sufferers were at best branded lazy or at worst called stupid whereas today it is more recognised as a genuine disability. I've never forgotten one particular teacher telling me I was thick and that I wouldn't even be able to get a job as a dustman (no disrespect to all hard-working refuse collectors, but it was meant as a deliberate insult). Her words played on my mind every time it became obvious how far behind my classmates I was and it

"Education is an admirable thing, but it is well to remember from time to time that nothing that is worth knowing can be taught."

Oscar Wilde

just seemed to confirm that what she said was probably true... For me, most days at school became an affirmation that I was stupid.

It's hard to explain to someone who doesn't have dyslexia what it's like. Apparently a dyslexic's brain doesn't have the same synapses connections as your average brain. Synapses are the little receptors that carry information around your brain thus making it more difficult for me to recall certain information. The best way it's been explained to me was, each time your brain processes the information it requires to read, it sends signals down tiny pathways to be processed, but because my brain doesn't have the same number of pathways as a normal brain it takes longer for me to process the information. As an analogy, if you need some milk you would walk to the nearest shop using the most direct route, but, because of a lack of pathways, a dyslexic's brain would take you on a major detour thereby taking much longer to get to the shop. In fact when I read I put so much effort into working out what each word says I lose the gist of what I am reading.

A good way to demonstrate how difficult I find reading is for you to turn this book upside down and then read it backwards. Of course you will be able to read the words but it will be slower because you will have to put more effort into recognising each individual word. By reading backwards, the words won't have any meaning or context. This is not completely accurate but it will give you an idea what being dyslexic is like for me. Even today, at 46 years old, the most humiliating thing I've ever experienced was having to read out loud in class with all the other kids smirking and sniggering. Yet this apart, my memories of school were mainly of having fun - which I suppose means either I have a built-in self-defence mechanism or I'm in denial.

You're probably wondering how I managed to get over my disability as I'm now writing this book. The fact is, I still have problems with reading and spelling, but I'm now proud of being dyslexic even though it held me back in my formative years.

"If you don't design your own life plan, chances are you'll fall into someone else's plan."

Jim Rohn

Fortunately, with modern technology and my trusty laptop, things are much easier. I can write e-mails, letters, and even this book with simple speech recognition programmes. I can just sit and talk to my computer and it writes down everything I say. I can also highlight any text and have the computer read it back to me. I used to be ashamed and embarrassed about dyslexia because of the commonly held view that it meant you were stupid – until I learned that people like Henry Ford and Richard Branson had also suffered from it and that myth was blown right out of the window! Or is that water?!

I now believe that dyslexia is one of my greatest assets. You know how people with a disability tend to excel in other areas? For instance, someone who is blind will often have heightened senses of touch and hearing... I know coping with dyslexia is nothing like the same as being blind, but being dyslexic made me become highly organised and I developed systems to simplify everything I do. This has helped me to become very time-efficient. Take a look at everything you do whether it's at work or at home and de-clutter it. Ask yourself 'Can I simplify this? Is there an easier way?' Most of the things we do in life are things we learnt from other people, so we often do them the way we do because that's how we were shown, whereas there may be a much more effective way of doing things - they just need a little thought.

I remember hearing a story once about a newly married couple; they had recently moved into their new home and were going to cook their first Sunday dinner. As the wife prepared a joint of meat for the oven, the husband noticed that she had carved a piece of what seemed perfectly good meat off one end of the joint. Not wanting to upset his wife, he carefully asked, 'Why have you cut off the end of the joint?' She replied, 'You always cut off the end of the joint before you roast it'. He thought it was a waste and during the meal they talked about the reasons why she did it. The only explanation she could come up with was that ever since she was a little girl her mother had always cut off the end of the joint before roasting. They decided to

*"Never!
Never!
Never give up"*

Winston Churchill

call her mother to ask her why! Her mother came up with the same reason; she'd always cut the end off a joint because that was how her mother had done it. So they decided to ring her grandmother and posed the same question. 'Hi Grandma, I asked Mum why you cut the end off a joint of meat before roasting?' She replied, 'That's simple, my dear. I only have a small roasting tray and it's the only way I could fit the joint in...' The moral of the story is obvious - don't accept everything you're shown as the only way.

The simplest of things can often be the most effective. I have always had a problem with losing my keys; I just seem to put them in the most random of places and then waste hours looking for them. I got so fed up wasting time looking for keys, and often being late for specific appointments, that I eventually came up with a solution. Place a dish on the hall table, so, as I came in to the house I would put my keys in the dish. This has now become a habit and has proved to be very effective. Since that time, I have probably saved hours, possibly days, in time looking for keys. I know this is a very simple example but where there is a problem there's always a solution. Don't just accept things the way they are.

There are many ways of being more efficient in our day-to-day lives and often you will save a huge amount of time. The more time you can save, the more time you will have for living! Remember, at the end of it all, time is the measure of true wealth. The thing that makes us truly rich is being able to afford to spend our time doing the things we *want* to do *when* we want to do them – and to achieve this we need to work less. Therefore we need to create an alternative to our pay cheque – and that's really what this book is about... **An alternative to your pay cheque.**

"It is what you learn after you know it all that counts."

Coach John Wooden

CHAPTER 2

My Real Education

I think one of the most valuable lessons I have learnt in life is the value of integrity. Without integrity, you have nothing. If someone cannot trust you or believe in you, you're going nowhere fast. I would never have been invited to get involved in the majority of projects, businesses and opportunities I've been involved in, without integrity. You'd probably even struggle to get a decent job. Unfortunately, I had to learn the lesson of integrity the hard way. One of my earliest entrepreneurial ventures into making money got me in to rather a lot of trouble. I'm not at all proud of this but I'm going to share it with you anyway.

I grew up in an English seaside town which attracted a huge number of tourists in the summer months and then was like a ghost town in the winter. This was back in the seventies and early eighties when foreign holidays were just taking off and the English resorts were still very popular. One of the things that you would always find in these sorts of towns were the amusement arcades with all sorts of game machines. Back then most of the machines would take a 10 pence coin to play. This was where an idea to make lots of money developed.

Living so close to the sea, my brother became a keen fisherman. He would even make his own fishing weights by melting down lead and pouring it into a plaster mould. This is what gave

"The only real mistake is the one from which we learn nothing."

Henry Ford

me the idea of making a plaster mould of a 50 pence coin and then filling it with water and freezing it. I then took my 50p shaped piece of ice and put it in the change machine at the amusement arcades. Unfortunately for me the machine made five clicks and with each click a shiny 10 pence piece dropped into the tray. The unfortunate bit will become clear later. But wait! I had just turned tap water into hard cash. I was so excited I spent the whole 50p on ice cream, then went to work making frozen 50 pence coins. I was able to make about 20 a day, but the only problem was, it was the middle of summer and my frozen money would often melt slightly and the machine would reject it. But ever resourceful I came up with a much more advanced way making 50 pence pieces.

Of course, at the time I wasn't familiar with terms like counterfeit and forgery; this was all to become clear later!!! Anyway, back to the new improved 50p. What I had devised was that by making a 10 pence coin slightly bigger, it would pass off as a 50 pence coin. Genius. So what I had come up with was that if I wrapped electrical insulation tape around the outside edge of a 10 pence coin and with a sharp blade trimmed off the excess tape it would pass off as a 50 pence coin. Even though it wasn't the same shape as a 50p it fooled the change machines. Bingo. I was now swapping 10p for 50p every go. 40p profit!!! In fact, two pockets full of taped up coins would need my school bag to carry my ill-gotten gains home. It wasn't long until the arcade staff were on to me. It was about day four into my new venture, I was putting coins in to the change machine when a man from the arcade came over and asked if I could wait while he reset the machine. I froze as he stood me to one side of the change machine, he then bent down and unlocked the drawer at the bottom of the machine. Quickly coming to my senses, I decided it was time to leave and legged it. I had never been so scared in my life and thought it was best to lay low for a bit. The next day I woke up with renewed vigour. No need to lay low, I would just go to the neighbouring town of Torquay; they had lots of amusement

"Formal education will make you a living; self-education will make you a fortune."

Jim Rohn

arcades there. That afternoon as I was walking home with two bags full of stolen coins, thinking how clever I was, a police car pulled up alongside me. That was the end of that!!!

I will never forget the look on my mother's face when the police invited her to come and pick me up from the police station. They explained to her I had stolen over £500 from the amusement arcades using fraudulent 10 pence coins that were covered in my fingerprints. I had a criminal record and I was only 16! I now believe I was lucky to be caught, as by getting caught I learned the consequences and by my early twenties I was a staunch believer in karma. What goes around comes around. What you put out there is what you get back.

My real education took place once I'd left school. In my early 20s I was given a recording of Earl Nightingale narrating "The Strangest Secret" which completely blew my mind. I then listened to Napoleon Hill's "Think and Grow Rich". That made me realise anything was possible. Where most people my age were listening to their favourite music, I was listening to people like Zig Ziglar, Anthony Robbins, Dale Carnegie, Jim Rohn and lots of other amazing educational material. (In fact, since then, I always listen to audio books in my car.) One of the biggest mistakes some of us are guilty of is stopping learning once we leave education – it's so important to keep feeding our minds and keep learning new things. All your success will have been achieved from the things you learn, so don't stop learning.

The difference between the education you have received at school compared with what you get from the school of life, is that at school we are taught to get things right and not to make mistakes whereas the school of life will teach us that we can learn as much from a mistake as we can from getting something right. You see, if I get something right I congratulate myself and move on. Alternatively, if I get something wrong, I will analyse it and work out where it went wrong and learn from this for the future. (Whereas at school we were programmed to get things right and taught that making a mistake was a bad thing

"The person who never made a mistake never tried anything new."

Albert Einstein

which was marked with a big red cross.) School education just teaches us to play it safe and not get anything wrong, which in turn just fuels our fear of failure. If you get something wrong you're more likely to avoid doing it again. Instead of this, if you are to take on board that there is no such thing as failure, just results, you will put yourself in the position where the fear of failure no longer applies. From now on look at everything from the point of view of that there is no such thing as failure, just a result.

One of the main reasons I wrote this book is because if I'd known at 21 what I know now, I could have achieved so much more in a FRACTION of the time! That's why I'm now passionate about sharing what I've learned. I would definitely attribute my success so far to the knowledge and direction that I have gained from all the audio books I have listened to over the last 25 years. In fact, there is one book that I bought when I was 35 which gave me more focus than any other, and it's now regarded as one of the most influential books in its field... "Rich Dad, Poor Dad" by Robert Kiyosaki. You may have heard of it.

I have definitely benefited from listening to some amazing information, although it has led me to want to offer something slightly different to much of the self-help motivational advice I've loved listening to in the past. You see, after listening to a great motivational speaker I've often found myself feeling really positive and raring to go – but I always found myself wanting more than feeling upbeat and positive. Part of this book will give you some practical steps you can take, whatever stage you are presently at in life, but before we get to that, let me tell you a bit more about my background so when I say *'If I can do it, anyone can'* you'll understand where I'm coming from!

When I left school I started an apprenticeship in engineering. My father is an engineer and, as I was better at practical tasks than academic ones, it seemed a good route to follow. I soon realised that working in a factory in oily overalls with

*"Belief in oneself is
one of the most important
bricks in building any
successful venture."*

Lydia M. Child

not much to show for it other than grubby fingernails wasn't for me. Within a year of leaving school, I had ditched my apprenticeship and had started as a trainee (okay, a labourer) in the building industry, and within two years I was able to buy my first house. I was 18 years old. Always one for a challenge, I bought the house for £19,000 and sold it 18 months later for £29,000, having spent about £2,000 on materials and undertaking the renovation myself. Thinking back, that little house was definitely what sparked my passion for property.

I had only had a couple of jobs at this point and soon realised that I didn't make a very good employee! I'm stubborn, I like to do things my own way, and I'm also not very good at taking instruction (all coping strategies I learned to survive at school while being dyslexic). By the time I was 20, I was self-employed in the building industry installing double glazed windows and by the time I was 23 I'd set up my own business with the ambition and focus to create a company of great value so that I could sell-out for millions and retire in the lap of luxury. Although things didn't quite work out like that (in fact I've never made more than a reasonable income from the businesses I've owned) the thing that really made me wealthy is what I *did* with that income...

Most of us are taught to work hard at school to get a good education so that we get a good career, which in turn will give us a good income. The big problem with this is that at no point are we taught what to do with that income. We've all been led to believe the bigger your earnings, the wealthier you will be, but the truth is that the more we earn usually the more we spend on the things we desire. Most of the people I know who earn six-figure incomes have the nice house, the car, the holidays and so on – and they need every single penny they earn to support that lifestyle!

What I want to show you can be achieved on just an average income. It might take a little bit longer but once you get going, the amount of money you earn becomes irrelevant. You see

*"The only way to
enjoy anything in life
is to earn it first."*

Ginger Rogers

if you were to implement my plan from the time you leave education, most people would be able to retire at around 40 rather than the typical 60 to 65 – which is gradually being moved to even older than that and on less money per week than it takes to fill your car with fuel! I was able to retire at 44. This wasn't something I had intended to do but in 2008 when the world recession really took hold, my property developing business ground to a halt. Not only were banks reluctant to lend money to fund new projects, but property prices began to fall and as a consequence homebuyers virtually disappeared. Obviously it was pointless building houses without a market to sell to. Fortunately for me, I had an income from rental properties that gave me the capability of sitting back and biding my time so I could work out what I wanted to do next and this is precisely what has led me to helping teach others how to become financially free. The point I'm trying to get across here is probably one of the most important things that we will cover - **It's not *what* you earn but what you DO with what you earn** that matters. (This is covered in detail in a later chapter.)

Too many of us reach retirement age and find we have to carry on working. More and more of us are losing faith in the traditional investment methods such as pensions. Most pensions leave us retiring on a lot less money than we have been used to earning. They rely on how the pension company's investments perform up until your retirement – and if you're still not sure why you need to be in control of your own financial future just look online at a pension calculator! It's depressing how much money you need to invest to achieve such little return. Now I'm not advocating that you don't have a pension because if you're not doing anything else it's got to be better than doing nothing, but the time has gone when we could rely on them to see us through our retirement years. You may have noticed that I'm a little bit negative about pensions? I've seen too many people reach retirement believing they would have a certain level of income that was sold to them at the time they took out a pension, but the reality is the income they receive is a fraction of what they had expected.

"An investment in knowledge always pays the best interest."

Benjamin Franklin

There is no reason why we should have to cut back on our lifestyle when we retire because our income has reduced. The investments that we make during our working life should grow and keep on growing and when we retire we should get richer, not poorer. This is perfectly possible to achieve if we get on the right track and create a solid plan for the future.

It's a fact that more and more of us are living longer and healthier lives, which is great news as long as you're not relying on a state pension. I can't comment on other countries but the UK state pension is comparable to an illegal Ponzi scheme. Let me try and explain what I mean as people often say I've gone mad when I say this, so please hear me out... a true investment is one where you would deposit your money with an organisation which works with your money to make more money. Agreed? The extra they make over and above your original investment is profit, which is used for reinvesting, paying the investors a dividend and making profits for the organisation etc. However, a Ponzi scheme is where you would unknowingly deposit your money with a bogus organisation which gives you a false return on your investment by paying a part of that original investment back to you, which of course makes you think the investment is doing well... as no investment profits are actually made though, the scheme relies on new investors' money coming in to pay existing investors out, and once the amount needed to pay those existing investors out is bigger than the new investment coming into the scheme it inevitably collapses.

So, how is this system similar to a state pension? Well, while most people think the government invests a proportion of their national insurance contribution for their future pension, the reality is that the government makes all pension payments with money raised from today's tax revenue. So even though today's pensioners have contributed to their state pension throughout the whole of their working lives, in effect, their money was spent long ago by previous governments. The only way left is for the country to pay out state pensions from the taxes we pay today. The problem with this though is that the longer we

"The philosophy of the rich versus the poor is this: The rich invest their money and spend what's left; the poor spend their money and invest what's left."

Jim Rohn

live the more people there are who can claim a pension, so the only way the government can afford to keep on paying is either by raising the rate of tax, or raising the age that we are eligible to claim, or lowering the pension payments. All bad news! Just like a Ponzi scheme, there is no actual investment made and the pay-outs are from today's contributors, and the only difference I can see is that although it's failing, it hasn't collapsed yet...

I don't know about you, but as I get older I want to be able to afford the things I want to do and have the time available to enjoy them. I don't want to constantly worry about what I can and cannot afford. To make sure you're not reliant on the present system, as I've said before, *you* need to take responsibility for your own financial future. Therefore we need to find investments that *you* are in control of – that *you* can easily manage – and that will grow in value and give you good cash flow. So that's what I'm going to show you and if I can do it, you can too.

I definitely *don't* think there are the rich, and then **I'm afraid,** there are the rest of us! This is definitely not the case. All of us are capable of achieving anything we set our minds to. I believe there's one fundamental difference between the wealthy and the poor, the haves and the have-nots, the rich and the rest of us... One simple thing that divides us – something that we all know about – but something we don't seem to know what to do about. So what is it? **The simple difference is that we work for money, and the rich have money work for them.** I'll say that again. **The simple difference is that we work for money, and the rich have money work for them.** And that's the simple truth of the matter.

Whereas we spend all of our income, the rich have some of their income making more income and the richer you get the easier this becomes. Now I know you're probably thinking that's because they have surplus money whereas most of us have no extra money. What we do have we need to live on and pay the bills. Stop worrying about that just now as there are some key steps that we will go through, taking you from working for money, to having money work for you, that will be covered in a future chapter of this book.

I also think it's important to determine what is meant by rich, because being rich can conjure up so many different thoughts and emotions for different people. For a lot of us 'rich' has nothing to do with wealth. Therefore I feel a need to separate the richness of life from being financially rich. This book is about accumulating assets and financial wealth, although the obvious irony is that being financially rich gives us the time to have a more fulfilled and a 'richer' life.

"Lack of money is the root of all evil."

George Bernard Shaw

CHAPTER 3

Money is easy

The first principle of wealth is to decide if you really want financial success. Then decide if you are prepared to take a different route to the typical financial life most people lead. Make a firm decision to join The Rich Revolution. The best place to start is with your present financial position and your thoughts and understanding about money.

You see, money is simply a tool, and just like any other tool you need to know how to use it whether you're well off or broke. Take a carpenter, for instance: he's probably a lot better at using a saw than I am because he's been taught how to use it. He understands that for it to be most effective he needs to keep it sharp and for this reason he needs to treat it with respect and use it properly. Also, he finds the more he uses it the easier it becomes, so he can now pick up a piece of timber and cut it perfectly square without even marking a line. Money is the same as any other tool and once you know how to use it properly it just gets easier and easier. This book will show you how to use money as an effective tool, how to take control of it so it doesn't control you, and how to make money make more money! To do this you first need to work out what your present beliefs are about money. So just pause for a minute and make some notes on what comes into your mind when you think of money.

"Never let someone who has given up on their dreams talk you out of yours."

Ty Cohen

Notes:

....

....

....

....

....

....

....

Okay, now you've done that, review what you've written down. Are they positive things, negative things, or maybe both? Whatever you've written, it doesn't actually matter because these are simply your thoughts and beliefs you have built up over the years. What does matter is that you can change your beliefs and present thoughts about money and create new beliefs and habits which will help you to deal with money. Remember, I need you to believe that money is merely a tool, that it's easy to control, and that it's simple to create. Now for you this may seem impossible to believe but once you understand the process it becomes much clearer. By the way, this will not happen overnight! You are going to have to put in some time and effort, and this will be an on-going process to learn what you need to know about creating wealth. For you this book may just be an initial step. However, if you are prepared to commit to educating yourself about how money works, you can look forward to a more prosperous future...

First of all it's important that you get your mindset right about money. You see, money is simply a mechanism that was invented to replace bartering, albeit there are some people who believe that money is the main cause of all the problems in society. The fact is it's the system that we have and until someone comes up with a better and more effective solution I'd suggest we work with the one we've got.

"Money is only a tool. It will take you wherever you wish, but it will not replace you as the driver."

Ayn Rand

As I've already said, money is merely a tool. It's easy to control and simple to create. The hardest one of these for most people to believe is that money is simple to create! Let me explain. Most people only think of money in its physical form as the notes and coins in your pocket – and most of us create money by going to work and getting paid a wage, which is probably the most popular way there is of creating money. This, I'm afraid, can often lead to one of the biggest problems in how we think about money. You see, most of us work hard for our income. This leads us to believe that creating money is hard work and if you don't change your belief, money will continue to be hard work. To change this belief, we need to accumulate some money and then set that money to work, and eventually your money will be doing the hard work. The biggest problem is that the majority of us spend all of our income; therefore we don't give ourselves the chance of getting to the stage where we could have our money working for us. Remember the difference between the rich and the rest of us; they have money work for them and we work for money.

What I need you to understand and believe is that money can be created and often from nothing more than an idea. There are millions of different ways that we create money - we just need to improve on, or widen, our present focus. Let me give you a few examples of the creation of money. Take Facebook or Google, for instance. It wasn't too long ago when they were no more than an idea. But from those ideas a huge amount of wealth has been created. Now I'm not saying you need to come up with an idea like Google – I'm just trying to explain how money can be created. Although if you do come up with the next Google that would be amazing.

Another example could be that you have a piece of land and you build a house on it. Let's say the land is worth £200,000, it costs £200,000 to build the house, and the finished value of the project is £500,000. You have created £100,000 that didn't exist before the house was built. One more example. You put £1,000 into an investment that pays 10% per year so that at the end of

*"Put your money into land.
They're not making
it anymore."*

Abraham Lincoln

the year your £1,000 is now worth £1,100. In this case whatever you invested in has paid you for the use of your money and you have created £100. This is all very obvious stuff but how often do you put time aside to think about how to create more money? Just remember, money is simple to create. If you can understand this principle and it is different to your previous beliefs you have already started to expand your ideas about money.

Just to take the idea of creating money one step further, let's go back to the example of the piece of land worth £200,000. In the process of building the house at a cost of £200,000, much of this money will have been paid to various tradesmen to complete the finished house. So not only has the house created £100,000 worth of value, it has also created £200,000 worth of income for all the various tradesmen involved in building the house.

Therefore you need to change your mindset and believe that money can be easy to create. In fact there is an abundance of wealth to be created, it really is limitless. This is an important step to creating wealth and by committing to reading this book and deciding to be different, you are already well on the way to success. If you are interested further in the practical steps laid out in this book, you might wish to look at the Wealth Creation Program that has been designed around the principles you are reading about. It includes interactive software and a simple step-by-step guide to help you through things like debt reduction, money allocation and obviously investing for wealth creation.

So now that you've got some positive thoughts about money, let's look at the reasons you need to understand why you want a secure financial future. They may seem obvious but it's very important for your success to be able to visualise how your future will look, where you'll be living, how financial security will make you feel and all the ways your life will change. Your personal reason is so important because it's what will give you the direction and purpose that will become the foundation of your plan. The first practical step you need to undertake is to create that plan. There are lots of things we do that we wouldn't dream of attempting

"An idea not coupled with action will never get any bigger than the brain cell it occupied."

Arnold H. Glasow

without some in-depth planning. For instance, we wouldn't dream of getting married without often up to a whole year's forward planning. Moving house – again, a lot of organisation and planning. A family holiday – I could go on – but my point is we are forever planning and organising individual parts of our lives, yet most of us omit to plan for what we truly want out of life! Like I've already mentioned most people leaving education today are more than capable of becoming financially free from work by the time they are 40 but we know what it's like when we're young and we think we're immortal! In reality, of course we're not, and nor do we know what life is going to throw at us...

Creating a plan gives you an effective route to follow. This will keep you on track and stop you from deviating down the wrong path. To help you I have come up with a very simple formula to build your plan around. The What Formula! - that's not a question it's the name of the formula...

'The W.H.A.T Formula'

It stands for 'Why, How, Action & Time'. Success comes from doing something well and to do something well you first need a good reason **WHY** to do it. Then to accomplish whatever it is you want to undertake you need an effective method i.e. **HOW**. Having a good reason 'why' and a method 'how' will motivate you to take **ACTION**. Finally, the success you achieve from your actions will lead to **TIME**. Giving you freedom from having to work for money. This will form a framework for your plan. Your reason why will give you goals and targets to focus on. This book and other learning materials will teach you how and what you need to do and your plan will be a list of actions that you need to undertake to get from where you are now to time freedom.

So remember this simple formula to help build your plan.

(W + H) x A = T

Reason **WHY** + Method **HOW** x **ACTION** = **TIME** Freedom

"Wealth is the product of man's capacity to think."

Ayn Rand

As I have already said, we all need to take responsibility for our own future. I really believe that. I hear so many people moaning about situations around them which they have no control over or any way of influencing, such as the economy, the price of fuel, cutbacks, interest rates, inflation, etc. You only have to watch the news to see the endless barrage of negativity. We would all be so much better off if we just focused on our own *personal* economy and how we could work at reducing our debt and improving our income, and, as I said, take responsibility for ourselves instead of getting caught up in other people's problems that we often have no way of solving. If you want to break your present cycle and create a more positive situation in your life your reason **why** is vital to help you achieve this. By creating a plan that clearly lays out the things you want out of life, you will have a clear and positive route to follow.

Initially, there are some key things about your plan that you must understand for it to work effectively and ensure your future success. So that your plan is tailored to you and for it to give you true purpose and direction, you need to ask yourself two very simple questions.

Firstly, 'Exactly what is 'wealthy'?'

Secondly, 'Why do I want to be wealthy?'

Now you're probably thinking the answers are obvious and that being wealthy is having a lot of money, and the reason you want lots of money is so that you can have and do the things you desire. Although this answer isn't wrong, it's not the answer we're looking for. You see, to become really wealthy doesn't happen overnight – it takes time and effort – so to make sure you put in that time and effort you need a plan to give you focus. If becoming rich was easy, everyone would be rich! The things we need to achieve to become wealthy are relatively simple but without the plan and a strategy to follow, things will become muddled and you will lose your way. So let's get back to those two questions because the answers need to be fully understood before you can create an effective plan.

"Though I am grateful for the blessings of wealth, it hasn't changed who I am. My feet are still on the ground. I'm just wearing better shoes."

Oprah Winfrey

CHAPTER 4

What is 'wealth'?

To understand what wealth is, we need to be able to measure it. The reason we need to measure wealth is that different people have their own expectations from life and everyone's criteria will be different. Some of us will want to live a five-star luxury lifestyle and others would be happy with no possessions at all. Neither of these is right or wrong – it's just very important that you know what you want because this will create such an important part of your plan. It's virtually impossible to achieve something really worthwhile without something to aim at and this is what creates your focus.

QUESTION: IF YOUR INCOME STOPPED TOMORROW – HOW LONG UNTIL THE MONEY RUNS OUT? A YEAR? A MONTH? A WEEK?

Let's face it – most of us already know there's too much month left at the end of the pay cheque – and that's the REAL measure of your wealth. Contrary to popular belief, your wealth is not equal to your possessions or lifestyle. Your wealth is not proportional to your income. In my experience, your wealth is proportional to the length of time you can keep your current lifestyle if your income stopped tomorrow. If you were able to expand your lifestyle, i.e. have more money in any given month coming into your household than the previous month, without your earning ability, you would be truly wealthy. In

"Birthdays are good for you. Statistics prove that the people who have the most live the longest."

Larry Lorenzoni

other words, if your income went up every month, even if you didn't go to work, you'd have the sort of wealth I'm talking about.

So how do we measure wealth?

It's simple, like most things I do. The simpler something is, the easier it is to do and the more likely we are to do it! **We measure wealth by working out how long you could survive financially if your income suddenly stopped**... For instance, if you need £5,000 a month to live the lifestyle of your choice, and had to stop work and had £10,000 of savings, you'd only be able to sustain your lifestyle for two months. Therefore, in this scenario you would be wealthy to the level of two months. Your wealth is measured by the length of time you can exist on the money you have available, not the amount of money you have. To become totally financially free, you would need to accumulate enough wealth to last you the rest of your days. In other words, if you needed £5,000 per month, you would need £60,000 a year and if you have 50 years to live, you would need £3 million to survive the rest of your days in the lifestyle that you've chosen. Now I know this is very simplistic as it hasn't taken into account the interest on the £3 million, or inflation over the next 50 years, and many other factors – but just the practicalities of accumulating this amount of wealth is beyond most of us.

What's the answer?

Well, you need to create a £5,000 a month income that doesn't require you to work. Simple! In other words, you need to create a 'passive' income – and this is the difference between the rich and the rest of us.

We work for money, and the rich have money work for them.

For the purposes of our plan, we need to work out how wealthy we are right now to give us a starting point. We will come to how to create a passive income later. We need to work out the

*"Dost thou love life?
Then do not squander time,
for that is the stuff life is
made of."*

Benjamin Franklin

lifestyle we desire and from this we can calculate the amount we would need per month to achieve it. This becomes the target passive income of your plan. Your plan will thus be built up of things you need to achieve and put in place to create the passive income to support the lifestyle you desire. For this strategy to work, you first need to understand your end goal. Your plan is like a journey and like any journey you need to work out your route, but you cannot work out a route unless you first have a destination. The first exercise for your plan is to understand where you are starting from and where you want to end up, and like any journey once we know the start and finish point we then simply work out a route between the two.

If you ask most people what the definition of being rich and wealthy is, 90% of the time the answer is 'lots of money!' whereas in fact it's actually 'lots of **time'**. Hopefully you're beginning to understand that the definition of wealthy is having enough passive, unearned income so that you can **afford** your lifestyle and more importantly - **have the time to enjoy it**.

To illustrate this, some time ago I went through a pretty difficult period in my life – I was financially better off than I had ever been, but emotionally I was unhappy. I used to confide in a good friend and it didn't take me long to realise that what he had was what I wanted. You see, I had been busy working hard to accumulate all the things I wanted out of life – I had a great house, nice cars, and my pride and joy - a 40 foot long Sunseeker sportsboat in our local marina with a jet ski and all the toys. I earned a good income from my businesses and I also had an income from developing property and another from my rental property portfolio.

But none of these things were giving me the happiness that my friend had. On the face of it he seemed like any other guy – he had an average income and a nice home – but crucially he had worked out that time and what you do with it is the most rewarding thing of all. He worked hard during the winter months and put money aside to see himself through

*"It's not what you earn,
it's what you do with
what you earn."*

Bruce Bishop

the summer months. Being self-employed he could choose the hours he worked, so when his kids were on their summer holidays during that five to six week period he wouldn't work much and it didn't matter – he'd spend it with his family doing the things he wanted to do and he was really enjoying life.

Although he wasn't completely time free as he still had to work hard during the winter months, he was living a much more fulfilled life then I was! This taught me a huge lesson about how precious time really is. Up until that point, most of my life had been spent working extremely hard and often very long hours, all to accumulate the things I believed would make me happy, yet I soon realised by learning from my friend that **time** is really our most valuable commodity. It's only the time we have doing the things we want to do with the people we love that really counts. How we feel is so much more important than any material possessions we have, therefore we should want to be wealthy in order that we can be **time free**.

To answer the question, "What is wealth?", the true definition of wealth to me is having time, but having lots of time without money leaves you unable to afford the things that we want to do with our time, so there's a balance that we need to achieve. Therefore most of us will fall into one of the next four categories of time/wealth:

1. You have a small amount of time available and little money.

2. You have lots of time available but very little money.

3. You have very little time but lots of money.

4. You have lots of time and lots of money.

"Never underestimate the determination of a kid who is time rich and cash poor."

Cory Doctorow

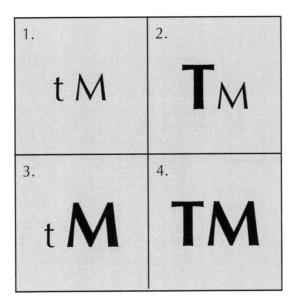

Obviously the fourth category would be most people's ideal but let me go through each of them and see where you are at the moment.

1: You have a small amount of time available and little money.

I think most of us fall into this category where we have a full-time job and work hard for an average wage. This leaves us in a position where we don't have a great deal of money or very much time because of our hours of work.

2: You have lots of time available but very little money.

It could be that you only work part-time, you may be retired on a pension, or maybe you're in the unfortunate position of being out of work for whatever reason. Any of these situations would mean you receive a small income or state benefits. Again, a less than ideal situation of having lots of free time but struggling to make ends meet.

3: You have very little time but lots of money.

Most of the people I know who fall into this category earn a very good income but they have to work very hard and often

"Know the true value of time; snatch, seize, and enjoy every moment of it. No idleness; no laziness; no procrastination; never put off till tomorrow what you can do today."

Lord Chesterfield

extremely long hours to achieve that, and therefore they don't usually have the time to enjoy their own wealth!

4: You have lots of time and lots of money.

This is obviously an ideal situation where you have created a good passive income and your time is your own. This would enable you to do the things you want to do, when you want to do them, and crucially, be able to afford it.

This should be an important part of your plan. It doesn't matter what category you currently fall into but it is important knowing where you are now and where you want to be so that you can focus on becoming time and money free. To achieve this freedom your plan needs to be a clearly laid out route from your present position to your future passive income... I found myself well and truly stuck in section number three and would probably still be there, working hard to cover the cost of all my luxuries without this plan. It was only through implementing the principles in this book that I've managed to reach section 4, and it's strange that some of the things that give me the most pleasure now cost virtually nothing. Things like taking my younger son to school in the morning and being able to pick him up later. These things don't cost much money but when my older son was at primary school I just couldn't have afforded the time to take him, I was too busy working hard.

You probably already know in your head what sorts of things you'd do if time was no object, if you weren't tied to your job. If you haven't thought about it, imagine you've just won the lottery. What would you do each day? Where would you live? What places would you like to see? What car would you drive? Maybe you'd like to do something to help others, whether that's family or a charity. Myself, I have a long list of things I want to do and see in my life. It's an amazing feeling, waking up in the morning knowing that my time is my own. Life can and should be a holiday!!! Hopefully all this is giving you some ideas about the sorts of things you can enjoy when you're financially free, all things that you can incorporate in

"Create a definite plan for carrying out your desire and begin at once, whether you are ready or not, to put this plan into action."

Napoleon Hill

your plan. But remember, you must write these down and review them regularly. The more you think of these things and focus on them, the more you will attract them into your life.

I'd like to tell you the story about the magic bank account. I've heard this story a few times over the past 20 years. The first time I heard it I probably didn't pay enough attention to the true value of its message, but as I get older it becomes more and more relevant.

You need to imagine that you have been given a magic bank account. This bank account is different to what you're used to, as it has no overdraft, it has no cheque book or cards, and it doesn't even have a bank manager. The unique thing about this account is it gives you the facility to withdrawal £1,440 cash every day. That's £10,080 per week, which is over £500,000 a year. You're not required to do any work for this money; it's given to you free of charge every day for the rest of your life. Also you can spend it in any way you like; the only stipulation is that you must spend all of it every day, because what you don't spend will be wasted. At midnight every night, the bank account is zeroed, a new £1,440 will be deposited for the next day and you can choose whether to invest or squander the money. The secret of this account is everyone has one in real life; it's just that the account isn't filled with money. Instead it's for usable minutes, and you have 1,440 minutes in every day, so invest them wisely. Money can be made, spent and made again but time can only be spent, so make the most of it...

When you create your plan, your long-term focus should be to have enough unearned passive income to support your dream lifestyle. Imagine being able to do whatever you desire. This is why understanding the reasons you want to be wealthy are so important, and yet most people still never create a life plan. Most businesses will have lots of systems and plans in place that are focused on them being successful, such as a mission statement, growth targets, sales analysis, stock control, strict budgeting and accounting - the list is endless. If we ran our own personal lives more like a successful business, we would achieve so much more. I don't mean that we need to be rigid and boring, but know where you're going and why. You really need to understand yourself and work out what you want out of life.

Therefore if the answer to 'what is wealth?' is being time free from having to work, and being able to afford the lifestyle you desire, then the answer to the question 'Why do I want to be wealthy?' must be so you can acquire the tangible things that you desire, to make your lifestyle a reality.

"In the absence of clearly-defined goals, we become strangely loyal to performing daily trivia until ultimately we become enslaved by it."

Robert Heinlein (1907-1988)

CHAPTER 5

Why do I want to be wealthy?

Now this is going to be very personal as we all have our own reasons and desires. Think about the lifestyle you would like to create and if you have a partner it's obviously worth working together so you can help each other achieve both your goals. It's the things you really desire that will give you true direction and purpose so put some quality time aside and some serious thought into what you truly want out of life. This can often be one of the hardest things to work out, but it is crucial that you do, because without having a direction or purpose you're basically drifting around going nowhere. It's like the comparison between a ship with an experienced crew with modern navigation equipment out at sea, and a piece of driftwood. The ship will get to where it's going because it has a well charted route and a reason for getting there, whereas the driftwood will just bob about and end up wherever the tide takes it.

One of the main reasons for a life plan is to control one of the most powerful of human emotions. The emotion I am talking about can be a double-edged sword and if you don't take control of it, it will often take control of you. If you control it, it can give you everything you ever wanted out of life. The emotion I'm talking about is desire. These days the amount of advertising and marketing we're exposed to is incredible. We are bombarded with things for us to want and desire. It's

*"Let us not seek to fix
the blame for the past.
Let us accept our own
responsibility for the future."*

John F Kennedy

everywhere we look; the press, television, the internet and just walking down the street. These modern marketing techniques are designed to raise your desire by painting a picture of the perfect lifestyle.

Unless you take control of your emotions, you will end up squandering any money you managed to accumulate on the latest thing that you want. This is usually a short-term fix as within a couple of months the item that you purchased has become part of the furniture and your desire for it has faded, that is until something else catches your eye. Without a plan or method to obtain some of the things that you desire, you can end up making feeble excuses and blaming others for not having the things in life you wanted, and this will often destroy your ambitions and leave you in a state of acceptance. Without a plan, most of what you want from life ends up as merely wishful thinking.

How do we control our desire? Well, one of the big differences between the rich and the rest of us is most wealthy people will look at things long-term whereas the rest of us mostly focus on the short-term or now. For instance, say your desire is to have a new kitchen, as your existing one is looking a little bit dated and could only be described as adequate. You put some thought into the layout and style you'd like, you research a number of kitchen suppliers and work out how much it's going to cost. You can now make one of two decisions; the first one is short-term thinking and the second is long-term thinking.

Firstly short-term, you decide to take out a loan and within a month the kitchen fitters arrive and within six weeks you have a beautiful new kitchen. A much more effective way, would be delayed gratification or long-term thinking. You place the kitchen in your plan as an item that you would like to afford in two years' time, and remember, your existing kitchen is adequate. Two years later, you have created some secondary and passive income as part of your plan and this extra income more than covers the cost of your loan that pays for the kitchen.

"If you buy things you do not need, soon you will have to sell things you need."

Warren Buffett

This way, you haven't added any extra burden to your income. By the kitchen becoming part of your plan, you controlled your desire, in that you knew you were getting the kitchen, and when, as this was set out clearly in your plan, instead of getting yourself further into debt and never giving yourself a chance to accumulate some funds that could be invested into something that could be making your money make more money.

Let's look at another scenario in that the kitchen you want costs £10,000 but in this scenario you have the £10,000 available in savings. You don't need to take out a loan; you simply spend your savings. Again, this is short-term thinking. The better way would be to find a good yielding investment in which to place your savings, then use the returns from your investment to make the payments on your kitchen. In this scenario, once you've paid down the loan you will have a great kitchen and you'll still have your savings. Hopefully this simple example will help you understand why controlling your emotions and desires is important, and how your plan is crucial in helping you do this.

Another benefit from this is that you will often end up with a much better deal and exactly what you want by taking your time. I'm sure all of us can think of a situation where you rushed into a decision and ended up regretting it. By the way, a small tip on getting a good price for something is to have more than one option and not to have to rush into a decision. Let me give you an example. When I'm looking to buy an investment property I will often have up to 10 or more properties shortlisted to make an offer on, and this helps me control my desire for any individual property. By having multiple options I don't have to worry about someone else bettering my offer and losing the deal. This way, I'm not led by my fear of loss and I'm able to negotiate from a position of strength, in that I have an alternative. I can then look at the properties from an investment point of view rather than getting too emotionally involved in the process.

Now we've got a grip on our desire we won't just run out and buy whatever we want without it being part of our plan. Although

"A goal properly set is halfway reached."

Zig Ziglar

we still need to create a list of the things we want and desire in our life, this will give us the focus we need to take action in turning that plan into reality. There are a number of ways of doing this. You can simply write a list, or you could write a few pages about where you'd be living, the sorts of cars you would be driving, the holidays you'd be taking and all the other things that would create the life you desire. This is often a lot more descriptive than just a list, although the method I prefer is a vision board, which is pretty self explanatory. It's where you pin up pictures on the board or create a gallery on your computer. I prefer this method as it's a lot more visual and easy to add to.

Back in my twenties, when I first started absorbing the information from audio books, virtually everything I listened to was saying I should focus on clearly defined goals. I remember being quoted some statistics from a survey of new university graduates who were just going out into the world of work. All of them were ambitious and were clear about what they wanted to do in life. But always the most successful by far, were the ones who had written down and constantly reviewed their goals and ambitions.

I was also told to stick up pictures of the things I desired because the more you visualise, think and focus on something, the more you attract whatever you need for it to become reality; it's called the Law of Attraction. Basically whatever you think about you will bring about in your life so if you think of lack and hardship, you will attract lack and hardship. Therefore if you think thoughts of being happy, healthy and wealthy, you will attract these things. If you have never come across the Law of Attraction before, I would seriously suggest that you read 'The Secret' by Rhonda Byrne.

When I first heard of the Law of Attraction, I struggled to believe it and for me to totally believe in something I need to see proof. I now find the best way to explain it is by comparing the human brain with a mobile phone. I don't need to prove to you that I can dial a number and within seconds be speaking

"Whether you think you can, or you think you can't – you're right."

Henry Ford

to someone virtually anywhere in the world. Not only that but millions of other mobile phone users are also talking to other people around the world without any of the calls getting crossed or mixed up. Now I confess that I don't completely understand how all these different frequencies can carry perfectly clear information backwards and forwards to millions and millions of individual mobile phone users but the proof is clear, it works. I could be speaking to you from the other side of the world or I could be speaking to you from just down the street, I have all the evidence I need that it works.

Now, if I was to ask you, which do you think is more advanced - the mobile phone or the human brain – I think most of us would agree that it's the human brain, it's incredible. I personally think that it's the most advanced thing on the planet, probably the most advanced thing in the universe. Who's to say when you think a thought that your brain isn't actually sending out a signal of that thought, not unlike a mobile phone? Scientists say there is over 90% of the human brain function they still do not understand, especially the subconscious mind. To me, the Law of Attraction is just like another law of nature. Take gravity, for instance. If you jump up, you come back down, you wouldn't expect to just keep going up. With the Law of Attraction, start thinking positive thoughts about the things you want in your life and keep on thinking about them and believe that you can have them. The Law of Attraction says, whatever you think about you will bring about, so be careful of what you think about. It's just like the old Chinese proverb, be careful what you wish for because you just might get it. In this case, be careful what you think about because you will get it. Make sure your thoughts are positive thoughts!!!

This can be quite challenging even for the most positive minded person. We all have that voice inside our head that we talk to when we're thinking things through. It wasn't until I started monitoring my thoughts that I realised how negative some of my thoughts were. In fact if the voice inside my head was a separate person I don't think I'd want to associate with

"Try not thinking of peeling an orange. Try not imagining the juice running down your fingers, the soft inner part of the peel. The smell. Try and you can't. The brain doesn't process negatives."

Doug Coupland

them. Once I started monitoring my thoughts I was amazed by the barrage of negativity that I would think of on a daily basis, worrying about bills I needed to pay, worrying about things going wrong at work, a constant stream of "what if this were to happen or what if that doesn't work, what if, what if, what if..."

Start monitoring your thoughts. Next time you're alone with your thoughts, maybe waiting for an appointment or travelling on your own, become conscious of your thinking and listen to the conversations you have with yourself. Then start to train yourself on thinking positive thoughts like, how great life is, how wonderful it is to be alive, what an amazing world we live in. Start visualising your perfect life, how it would make you feel, where you would live and actually see yourself living that life. I found the hardest thing about positive thought was remembering to think positive, so I came up with a solution. Every time I hear a telephone ring it would remind me to think, "More positive news for me". This might sound crazy but trust me, it works. One of the great tools that comes with the course that's been created to accompany this book is your own personalised life plan; by recording your positive thoughts and planning out the life that you would like to live and by constantly reviewing your plan, you'll be amazed as the things you want out of life become a reality.

So, by understanding that controlling your thoughts, emotions and desires by the use of a clearly defined life plan, hopefully you will understand why we need to have goals, rather than me just offering you statistics and saying do it because for some reason it works. Now remember, your plan isn't carved in stone, it's simply written on paper and it can change as your life changes. Your plan must be constantly reviewed and updated. A good structure for your plan is to have a 10 year long-term focus for your life, and a three year plan of action. Often our long-term goals can seem too big and unachievable, so to cut them down to size we concentrate on our short-term goals over the first three years. These three years can then be broken down into individual years, with year one being a plan

"One of the rewards of success is freedom, the ability to do whatever you like."

Sting

of action targeted at specific tasks. Year one can then be split into quarters, with the first quarter being divided in to three individual months. Eventually work back to what you need to achieve this week, and even break a week up in to a daily list of activities. This way you end up with a daily task list for every day until you reach your long-term goals, but you only have to plan the milestones and the tasks required for day one. It's actually very simple - just set yourself easy-to-achieve tasks and keep achieving!

By now you should understand that you need to create a plan, and why. To recap, you should have worked out your starting point. This is your present level of wealth and how long it would take before your money would run out if your income should stop. You also should have worked out what sort of lifestyle you would like to achieve 10 years from now as your long-term focus for the future. The next part of your plan is to work from your starting position to eventually achieve your long-term focus. Now 10 years is a long time and many things will change from now till then, including your plan. As I just said, it will and should evolve overtime so set yourself a few milestones along the way, let's say three, five and seven years. These should be things that you would like to achieve and would be a good measure of your success.

I believe that an important part of anyone's plan should be rewards. When you achieve something, reward yourself. You see, if all you ever do is work hard, pay off debt, save capital and invest for the future, life will become boring and mundane. For instance, say one of your initial goals is to pay off a credit card. When you achieve this goal, reward yourself; even if it's something as simple as going out for a meal, make the meal special and have a great time. You will then relate the achievement and success of paying off the credit card to the reward of the great night out, and, as your achievements become greater, so will the rewards. It goes without saying that your reward should be commensurate with your success.

"You cannot escape the results of your thoughts. Whatever your present environment may be, you will fall, remain or rise with your thoughts, your vision, your ideal. You will become as small as your controlling desire; as great as your dominant aspiration."

James Lane Allen

I remember one of my earliest successes when I renovated a small three-bedroom bungalow into a large four-bedroom house by converting the loft into a master bedroom with en-suite and converting an unused damp cellar area into a more usable living space. A great little project with a nice bit of profit but, unfortunately, I didn't have the investment knowledge I have now. I got carried away and spent all the profit on a new boat. The long-term benefits of reinvesting that profit into more income-earning activities would have been so much more beneficial for my future. In hindsight, I should have rewarded myself on a much smaller scale instead of blowing the whole lot on my short-term desire. This also taught me a valuable lesson on how much a money-eating liability boats are. This never quenched my desire for having a boat; I've had a few more since that first one, and the only difference is that I now put in place cash-generating assets to pay for my passion for boats.

For instance, if I were to buy a new boat today I would work out how much money it would cost to buy and how much money it would cost to run and then I would source an investment that would generate the amount of income required and then I would acquire the investment first, and buy the boat with the investment income. This way, you always stay ahead of the game. This is an important part of your life plan - don't forget to build in *suitable* rewards. Remember, life should be exciting and give you things to look forward to.

This throws up one of the most popular questions I'm asked. What should I invest in? As I'm not a qualified investment adviser, I can't give advice, although later in the book I talk about the investments that I have made that work for me!!! Even though I don't give specific advice on individual investments, this is where you can employ the strategy I talked about earlier - using experts. My personal expertise is in developing and investing in residential property, although I do invest in other areas such as start-up businesses, stock market and the foreign exchange market. In these investments I will use other people's expertise to help and advise me, thereby optimising my time.

I have also learnt some key fundamentals about investing through some of the audio programs I listen to.

As I've pointed out before, I'm not an all-knowing investment guru; most of what I have learnt about investing has come from others such as Warren Buffett, probably one of the greatest investors of all time. Some of the key points that he talks about are very simple and straightforward but make a huge amount of sense. For instance, only invest in something that you understand. This may take some learning on your part but will save you a lot of disappointment in the future. Another point he makes is: "Only invest in something that you are prepared to hold for at least 10 years", even if your plan is to make a short-term gain over six months. If things go wrong, would you be happy to keep the investment for the next 10 years? What I would be looking for in this situation is if the six month gain wasn't realised, then would the investment give me some cash flow over the next 10 years? 'Cash flow' is probably the most important part of wealth creation, which we will cover in the next section. You see, investing shouldn't be a short-term get-rich-quick exercise; it should be a long-term strategy for a secure future.

Hopefully you can now create your own personal reasons 'why'! This will give you a real focus and desire to create an exciting prosperous future. Now we need to concentrate on what *actions* we need to undertake to get our money working as hard as possible for us.

CHAPTER 6

HOW!

O kay, let's talk about the 'how'. What I'm going to go through is how to put in place the foundations for wealth. You see, there are millions of different ways to create wealth; I get bombarded with e-mails every day on different investment strategies in all different fields such as property, Forex trading, stocks and shares, and numerous business ideas. Whatever you end up doing to create extra income or cash flow is actually irrelevant to what I want to talk about. The point is first you must understand the foundations of wealth creation. Then, when you start building your wealth, you will know that it has a solid base to work from ensuring that the wealth you create will go on to create even more wealth. As I mentioned earlier, 'it's not what you earn, it's what you do with what you earn'.

Later in this section on how to create wealth, I'm going to talk about the strategies that I used to create a passive income, and why I still believe that property is one of the most secure, easy to achieve investments that there is, especially in the long-term. I will also share with you my seven reasons for investing in property. You will have to make up your own mind on the areas you would like to invest in, but that's for the future.

For now you only need to work out the next three years of your personal plan. This is clearly laid out in your own plan at the

"Home life ceases to be free and beautiful as soon as it is founded on borrowing and debt."

Henrik Ibsen

back of this book but before you create your own plan you need to clearly understand each section that takes you from where you are now to your long-term goals. And this is what we are going to cover next, the seven steps you need to take to get your money working for you.

The first step we have already covered, your long-term focus, your why, your passion, the thing that will drive you to take action. Step two I call **CASH FLOW!** This is understanding and taking control of your present financial position. The third step is money allocation; this is rearranging your existing budget using the **80-20 rule** that we will cover shortly. Next, is step four **GOOD!** Which stands for 'Get Out Of Debt', which is pretty self-explanatory. Then step five, **BUILD CAPITAL**, I call this your Wealth Fund! Then to secure the work you've achieved so far, step six is to create a **CONTINGENCY FUND** to protect your wealth against any unexpected events. Finally step seven, **INVEST** by using experts and other people's knowledge. I am sorry if this is sounding too simplistic to becoming wealthy but like I said all along, if I can do it, anyone can. The fact is most of us understand we should be doing something to provide for our future, but we're all too busy living our short-term lives to do anything about it. One of the greatest things about what I'm going to show you is it shouldn't have too much of an impact on your present standard of living and lifestyle.

Now if you're looking at this and you haven't got any debt, then you simply go straight to the next stage, and if you're fortunate enough to have some working capital, then as long as you understand all the stages and you have organised your income using the money allocation techniques, you'd obviously go to the final stage to start investing. Even if you are in the position where you have your money working for you and you're an experienced investor, the principles that I'm going to go through still apply. In fact, if you apply these simple strategies to your existing cash flow and investments, you will see a remarkable improvement in the way your returns compound.

*"Those who start with
too little money are more
likely to succeed than those
who start with too much.
Energy and imagination
are the springboards to
wealth creation."*

Brian Tracy

It doesn't matter where you are on the scale, you should always follow these basic rules of Money Allocation and rest assured, they are very basic and simple to achieve. You should even teach them to future generations, so once you've built your legacy you know it will always be in good hands. But before we cover Money Allocation, we need to have some money to allocate and if all of your present income is being spent, then you need to join The Rich Revolution and take these simple steps towards your own financial freedom.

Lets look at 'Cash Flow'. This to me is a key element to wealth creation. And the first thing to understand about cash flow is to ensure it is flowing in the right direction, in that you have more income coming in than you are spending. In other words, your income must be more than your expenditure. This is what we call positive cash flow and having worked out your starting point and your destination on your plan, this will be the first part of your journey. How much extra income you require over and above your expenditure, we will cover shortly in the money allocation section but for now we just need to understand that without positive cash flow, we are going backwards.

Now, this exercise is relatively straightforward but must be done accurately. You need to work out the total monthly income that is coming into your household; don't make any deductions, just add up the amount of money that you receive on a monthly basis. Then take at least your last three months' expenditure. This needs to include everything, so go through your bank statements, your credit cards, your cash purchases, right down to the coffee you buy on the way to work. Once you have at least three months expenditure, divide this by three to give you an average monthly expenditure. I have included a list at the back of the book to help you get this figure as accurate as possible. When you have these two figures, you take your expenditure amount away from your total income and what you have left is your monthly cash flow. This is the amount you have to work with to create your wealth. Obviously you are looking for your income to be bigger than your expenses, but

*"Never stop investing.
Never stop improving.
Never stop doing
something new."*

Bob Parsons

don't worry if it's not a lot, in fact don't worry if it's a minus amount, because if this is the case then you need to look at the areas where you can cut back on your spending. Alternatively you could create more income. Even if you have positive cash flow (where your income is greater than your expenditure), you may still want to look at generating more income. Obviously the more money you have available, the quicker you will reach your goals and achieve your plans.

I don't like cutbacks, I've never felt comfortable with skimping and scraping, therefore if I have a tight budget I would focus on creating more money, more positive cash flow, rather than cutting back on my existing lifestyle, but that's just my opinion, you will have to decide the best way for you. If I was to set you a task to research and find something you would enjoy, something that would create a secondary income, something you could educate yourself on, something that you could achieve in your spare time, I'm sure most of you could come up with something. The beauty of this is it doesn't have to be a large income, it just needs to top up your existing income to improve your cash flow.

All this aside, to create wealth you're going to need to allocate a percentage of your income for your investing. Remember, our focus is to get money working for us, to create a passive income, therefore we need to analyse the things you spend your money on. Most of us spend our money on our day-to-day living costs and then any surplus is mostly spent on the things that we desire. The problem is most of the things we desire end up going down in value. However, if we could control our desire and spending, we could start to divert a percentage of our income to things that appreciate in value and make us money. We could build towards a passive income without too much effect on our present lifestyle.

If you have money to spend, do you go shopping? Or do you have a plan for your future and look for something that can increase in value? The reality is that most people ONLY spend their income on things that decrease in value, ending up being worth less than what they paid for them. The more income they earn, the more they spend on these things, so we need to structure your spending to give us the lifestyle we desire as well as creating a passive income for the future. The way we define the difference between something that decreases in value and something that increases in value is simple. If it goes down in value or it costs you money (negative cash flow), then it's a liability. Whereas if it goes up in value or it pays you money (positive cash flow), then it's an asset and your focus should be on accumulating assets.

Your focus is to buy assets and have your money earn for you, just as an employee earns money for their employer. In fact, if you think of your money as productive employees, how many of them would you like to have working for you? Most of us work for money – we go to work and get paid a weekly or monthly wage. In other words, we are exchanging our time for money. We have a limited amount of time and therefore our earnings are limited to what we can charge for our time. If you employ your money correctly and buy assets, you can start the process of having it provide an income. No longer will your entire income depend on just your efforts. Can you imagine if your assets made more income than you? How would that make you feel? Well, that is exactly what it should do in time.

CHAPTER 7

Money allocation

The first time I heard about the strategies I'm going to cover, I was amazed how obvious they are and somewhat confused as to why I'd never heard this information before. Why had my parents never explained these simple rules? Why had I never been taught them at school? (Probably because I wasn't often there!) The fact is my parents weren't taught this in school either – and it's still not taught today. These principles aren't new – they've been around forever – but for some reason they seem to be largely ignored even though they are the fundamental principles of wealth creation. I've used the analogy before where I point out how a successful business would operate, and when it comes to money allocation, a business has some very effective accounting systems that we'd all do well to copy in our personal lives. Now, I know you may already be very organised with your money and you probably run your finances efficiently, but what is your strategy for your financial future?

I have always been reasonably good with money but the key strategy that turned my finances from a B- to an A+ was the rule of paying *me* first. What does that mean? Well it's as simple as it sounds – you must allocate a percentage of any money you earn to yourself before you pay anything else – and that means *anything* – be it your mortgage, your credit cards, your loans, your food bill or anything else you spend your money on. The

"My philosophy is that if I have any money I invest it in new ventures and not have it sitting around."

Richard Branson

money you pay yourself will become your 'Wealth Fund'. This might take some organisation and some getting used to, and obviously some commitment on your part, but trust me – *this is the key to your financial future*. If you don't commit to this fundamental principle, you will never have any surplus money working for you, and remember, the difference between the rich and the rest of us is that the rich have money working for them.

How much should you pay yourself to create your 'Wealth Fund'? I like to use the 80:20 rule. The Pareto Principle was developed and named after the Italian economist Vilfredo Pareto, who in 1906 observed that 80% of the land in Italy was owned by 20% of the population. After further research, he found that very similar percentages of land ownership occurred in most other countries and he developed his principle after observing that even 20% of the pea pods in his garden contained 80% of the peas!

This was one of the things I liked about the principle – it occurred in nature. For instance, in farming it was found that 20% of seeds sown yielded 80% of the crop. In business, Microsoft noted that 20% of the bugs in their programs caused 80% of the errors and crashes. Other research has shown that 80% of product complaints are caused by 20% of product. The thing that convinced me that the 80:20 rule works was when I realised that in a previous business I owned, virtually 80% of my sales came from 20% of my sales force, and that 20% of my marketing created approximately 80% of my leads. The following shows the 80:20 rule works with income as well. In 1992, the United Nations Development Program Report showed that the richest 20% of the world's population earned 82.7% of the world's income – and if the same research was done again today the figures would still be within a few percent of this. Now this may seem a little unfair – that 20% of us have over 80% of the wealth – but this only serves to drive me into making sure I'm in that top 20%!

"At least eighty percent of millionaires are self-made. That is, they started with nothing but ambition and energy, the same way most of us start."

Brian Tracy

One final statistic - 20% of people reading this book will act on the information and become financially free. 80% won't. Which group do you want to be in?

I don't completely understand why these percentages work but I know from the facts that the 80:20 rule is a sound principle and by using this principle you can create 80% of your wealth from 20% of your income. I'll say that again, 'Using the 80:20 rule, you can create 80% of your wealth from 20% of your income'. So how does it work? Well its simple; you take your total income and pay 20% of it to yourself first and then the remaining 80% is used to cover all your present living expenses. I mentioned earlier that you will be able to become wealthy without too much of an impact on your present lifestyle, and that's the sum of it – 20% of your income to become wealthy! Remember though, this is something you are going to have to do on a consistent basis and if it becomes difficult and painful to achieve then eventually you will give up. So it must be achievable, and you must reward yourself along the way, and you will find that it just becomes a way of life. In fact, it doesn't take long before it starts giving you an incredible sense of achievement, and brings a feeling of calmness and security to your life.

Taking 20% of your income to pay to yourself can often be a struggle, as a lot of us are already spending every penny we earn. Initially you may have to build up to 20% and this will become the next part of your Life Plan. As I mentioned earlier when talking about cash flow, you deduct your total monthly expenditure from your monthly household income and if there's not 20% of your income available to pay into your Wealth Fund, this leaves you two very simple choices... You must either cut your existing spending, or on a more positive note, create some extra income, or maybe a bit of both. As an example, let's say you have an income of £2,000 per month and all of this is spent on your monthly expenditure. In this example, your income matches your expenditure, therefore your cash flow is £0.

Now your task is to create 20% positive cash flow which initially can appear quite daunting, but if I was to say next month make a saving of 1%, that's just £20. Also in the same month, you need to generate an extra 1% income, and that's another £20. So in just one month, you will have generated £40 positive cash flow. Now if you could do that for 10 months, you will have created an extra £200 income per month, and in turn reduced your monthly expenditure from £2,000 to £1,800, saving another £200, giving you a total of £400 a month positive cash flow. This would be exactly the 20% that you required in just 10 months. At the end of the day, it all comes back to your why. Your reason why is what makes the initial transition bearable because if it doesn't, you need to re-address it. What is it that really drives you?

Let's cover an example of someone who is in debt; they still need to create 20% positive cash flow, so let's say they have a £5,000 loan, a £1,000 overdraft, and £3,000 on credit cards – a total of £9,000 debt as shown in the following example. I haven't included all debt in this scenario because the mortgage on their home is what I call 'good debt' in that it is acquiring them an asset. (If they're renting their home, they're not buying an asset; they're buying their landlord an asset!)

As the next stage in becoming wealthy is to be 'GOOD' (Get Out Of Debt), their Wealth Fund would be invested in paying off their debt. Let's use the same income scenario as in the previous example of £2,000 per month. According to the 80:20 rule, they need to allocate £400 per month (20%) to their Wealth Fund, and initially this should be used to clear their most expensive debt – the credit cards. Once all their debt is paid off, the £400 a month is allocated to building capital which will eventually be invested.

DESCRIPTION	LOAN AMOUNT	MINIMUM MONTHLY PAYMENT
Loan	£5,000	£100 pcm
Bank overdraft	£1,000	£10 interest payment
Credit card 1	£2,000	£ 60 pcm \
		> £90pcm
Credit card 2	£1,000	£ 30 pcm /
TOTALS	**£9,000**	**£200 pcm on debt**

Now don't worry if you've worked out your monthly expenditure and you can't afford to allocate 20% initially because you can build up to this. Let's take the previous scenario, where the income is £2,000pcm (per calendar month) and after making as many savings and cutbacks as you could, expenditure is still £1,800 per month – leaving only £200 (10%) towards the Wealth Fund. This would still be targeted at the most expensive debt (in this case, the credit cards). Once this is paid off, you would then target the next most expensive debt (the loan) and so on until your debt is cleared. In this case, it would give you an extra £200 a month that was servicing your debt bringing your Wealth Fund up to £400 a month, which is the 20% that you were looking for.

Debt reduction can be a very complex issue and very stressful, but again the programme we have created puts the information in this book in simple-to-follow step-by-step processes. It also has specialist software to help you reduce debt in the quickest and most cost-effective way, targeting the higher interest loans first, making your money be the most effective it can be. By paying off your debt, the money you were paying towards your monthly debt repayments will now be allocated to your Wealth Fund, and whilst you were paying off your debt, if you have been able to develop a secondary income, this will have improved your cash flow, helping you achieve your goals even quicker.

Now your focus can turn to *building capital* – the next stage in becoming wealthy. The rules remain the same in that 20% of all your income goes into building capital. The same applies when you start investing. The income you generate from your investments must also have 20% allocated to your Wealth Fund. So as your total income grows, the 80% allocated to your lifestyle grows, and the 20% allocated to your Wealth Fund also grows. The cycle continues and your total income compounds and compounds, making you wealthier and wealthier. To understand how powerful compounding is and how your money will truly work for you, I will cover this later in more detail using an example of how £1 a day can make you a millionaire.

CHAPTER 8

Contingency Fund

There is another important part to how we allocate money. You also need to build a Contingency Fund. This will act as a cushion, a buffer between your monthly expenditure and your Wealth Fund. It is vital that you protect your Wealth Fund against any unforeseen circumstances. Unexpected events have a way of being... well... unexpected! This would be used if the fridge packs up, or your car breaks down – or to bridge living expenses if you lose your job or your income should stop for any reason. It shouldn't take a crisis to make us realise the importance of a Contingency Fund.

I remember back in 1996 receiving a telephone call from a very nervous and uncomfortable customer asking whether it was possible to cancel the replacement windows he had ordered from my company a month or so previously. His situation had changed dramatically overnight. He was really concerned about whether he would be able to pay for his order because he was a farmer caught up in the BSE ('mad cow') crisis that had hit the UK and led to the European Union banning exports of British beef with effect from March 1996. That ban would last for 10 years. Because of the link to CJD in humans, the UK government decided that the only way to eradicate BSE from cattle was to slaughter all cows over a certain age. My customer and his livelihood were devastated. Suddenly, through no fault of his own, a hard-working man who had been running the farm that had been in his family for generations was about to lose everything. We really don't know what life has in store for us and that's why I believe having a contingency plan is vital.

Another situation closer to home involved my stepfather Don. I remember in the late seventies when my mother met him. He was an impressive person, especially to an impressionable teenager. I mostly remember being wowed by his sports car! He worked in personnel for a large American construction company called Bectel working in the oil-rich nations of the Middle East such as Saudi Arabia, Bahrain, Kuwait and Iraq. He earned an extremely good income for that time and had what seemed to me such a glamorous lifestyle to go with it, flying backwards and forwards on Concorde, eating out most nights, and he always had a big wedge of cash in his breast pocket! (It's funny the things that impress you as a kid.)

To cut a long story short, Mum married Don and I soon had a new brother. Fast forward to 1990 when Iraq invaded Kuwait which precipitated the first Gulf War. Saddam Hussein detained hundreds of citizens of Western countries who were working there and used them as a 'human shield' to deter military action against Iraq. At the time, Don was working in Baghdad and with a few other colleagues, made a dash for the British Embassy where they lived out the ordeal with around 70 other hostages. They kept themselves fit by digging trenches in the grounds of the embassy and occupied their minds by planning an escape across the desert. One of the initial problems was that the embassy had never been equipped to house 70 people! So they organised night sorties on nearby empty buildings to get provisions and equipment such as fridges and bedding, and they built makeshift tents to improve sleeping conditions.

Back home my nine-year-old brother would ask questions about the warplanes and the tanks on the TV and we'd reassure him as best we could. Mum put on a brave face as she always did and just refused to accept that anything tragic was going to happen, relying heavily on her Christian faith and praying hard.

Then Saddam Hussein announced he was going to release all foreign nationals, which was great news but he had lied about so many things up to that point that we hardly dared believe it. Bectel was amazing throughout the whole crisis though. They constantly relayed positive information and then at the end they flew all the hostages' closest relatives to Heathrow Airport. They put us all up at the Hilton and laid on the most amazing banquet to distract us while we waited for news... As long as I live, I will never forget the roar – like the winning world cup goal or a home run – that swept through the hotel when the announcement came that the hostages' plane had left Iraqi air space. By the time we heard our loved ones – the hostages – running down the flight of steps leading down into the hotel, emotions were at breaking point.

But to come back to my point – none of us really ever knows what life is going to throw at us. Unfortunately for my parents, the euphoria of that night came hand in hand with the realisation that it was also the end of a high earning career for Don. Unfortunately, they are no different to the majority of us in that they hadn't provided adequately for their future, and although they live comfortably, they now live a much more modest lifestyle than in the days of eating out and flying on Concorde.

So having some contingencies in place for whatever life may throw at us has got to be a good thing, and although there is always insurance to help us through unforeseen situations such as sickness, accidents and even death, it never covers everything – and let's be honest – how many of us can afford to have adequate insurance for all eventualities? The farmer I just talked about managed to scrape through the crisis and was eventually paid some compensation, but he definitely came out of the whole situation having lost a lot of money and ended up working a lot harder for a lot less than he had prior to the BSE situation.

As for my stepfather, I don't know if there are many insurance policies that would ever have covered that situation, and

"*Insanity: doing the same thing over and over again and expecting different results.*"

Albert Einstein

although his company carried on paying him during the time he was a hostage and for a period of recuperation afterwards when he returned home, eventually the work he used to rely on dried up. As we all know, international trade in Baghdad hasn't been thriving for some time.

Whatever unexpected events may occur, your Contingency Fund will be there so you don't raid your Wealth Fund. This should be the equivalent to at least six months' income. Now don't worry if you can't see a way of affording to put in place a Contingency Fund, it may take several years and that's OK; this is why you have a Life Plan! Your Contingency Fund can be something you set as a target for the future as part of building towards achieving financial freedom. You may be fortunate enough to afford to action this straight away but we are all different. One way of having a contingency without having to save up towards it is using credit such as an overdraft or even using credit cards, although I would only do this if you have the discipline to pay it off as soon as possible. Also a contingency must only be used in the event of a true emergency, for instance you wouldn't use it to go on holiday or to just go shopping, it must be kept for something unexpected like your car breaking down. It must only be used for something that is essential in your day-to-day life. It's these unexpected costs that can make it hard to afford the 20% you're paying yourself; that's why a Contingency Fund is vital to protect your Wealth Fund. Like I just said, you may not be able to afford to put in place your 20% Wealth Fund and the six months income contingency straight away, but as long as you are doing something and building up to this you are taking control of your own future rather than leaving it to chance. I've said it before – this isn't Get Rich Quick – the wealthy think long-term and the rest of us think short-term, and I can guarantee you one thing – *if you want things to change, you must make some changes!*

Just to clarify about your Contingency Fund. I would suggest that you still pay off your debt first before you start to build it. So, if you are in the position where you have some debt, but are fortunate enough that you can still afford your present lifestyle and pay yourself your 20% Wealth Fund, I would use your 20% Wealth Fund to pay off your debt first – the quicker you pay off debt, the quicker you stop paying interest and start earning it, and remember that's bad debt, not good debt like your mortgage – you can pay that off later. The most important thing is that you stick to the 80:20 rule, or as I like to refer to it, 'The 80:20 Law'. It doesn't matter how you get there, this will become clear in your Life Plan, what really matters is that you **must** get to the stage where your income is being split 80:20.

A quick recap on what we've just been through. First you need to create a strong reason why! To give you focus and to keep you on track, this should be based on replacing your present earned income with a passive income to the level of the lifestyle that you desire. This will become the target destination of your plan. You then need to work out your current financial position; this gives you a start and finish point on your plan. Then simply by changing the way you manage your money using the 80:20 law, you can sort out your **Cash Flow**, be **GOOD** get out of debt, **Build Capital** by creating a Wealth Fund, put in place a **Contingency Fund** for any unexpected events and finally **Invest** to get your money working for you, so eventually you will no longer have to work for money and you can experience true financial freedom where time is your own and you will have the rest of your life to enjoy the freedom that this brings.

The most amazing thing about your life plan is that most people can achieve this financial freedom from their present income. You now know all that's required is to reorganise the way you allocate that income. You already spend it on bills and distribute it across all your expenses. All you have to do now is distribute it in a different way, by paying yourself 20% first, before you pay anything else. This will set you free. Unless you need to create some extra income you should be able to achieve this with minimal effort, then, once you're in a position to start investing you just need to do some research and start employing experts to make your money work hard for you.

CHAPTER 9

Concentrate on your own economy

Before we look at how you start investing your Wealth Fund, let me just cover the investments that have worked for me and some of my thoughts on the subject. The main investment strategy I have used to build my wealth is property. As I've already mentioned, I am passionate about property; whether it's renovating a rundown property or developing a piece of land, I enjoy the whole process from negotiating the initial purchase to the end product, whether it's to rent or sell. I feel it's more like a hobby than a business. Richard Branson says in his book 'Screw It, Let's Do It', that he wouldn't get involved with a business venture unless it sounded fun and he was going to enjoy it. We are so much better at things we enjoy, I'm sure all of us can think back to subjects at school. We were always better at the ones we liked than the ones we disliked, this is the same in anything we do. Now you may be stuck with a mundane job that you don't enjoy but, by putting these strategies to work, your day job is only temporary. Just remember though, that the income from your job is your cash flow, and it's from your cash flow that you are going to build your wealth.

Before the recession of the early nineties I had converted a couple of properties into flats and sold them for profit. At this point the idea of renting property hadn't entered my head until around 1991 when I bought a two-bedroom terraced

"If a building looks better under construction than it does when finished, then it's a failure."

Doug Coupland

cottage for £40,000 that was in need of renovation. I spent around £4,000 on the renovation and undertook most of the work myself. During the summer of 1992, having completed the refurbishment, I had the property ready for sale. The only problem was that back in 1992 the UK was in recession and property prices had slumped, so it was at this point that I was forced into renting property although I'd never intended to become a landlord.

I decided to refinance the property to release the £4,000 I had invested in the renovation. To my shock the banks valuation came in at £38,000, £2000 less than I had paid for it and then, when you add the renovation costs, that's a loss of £6,000. There was no way I was going to be able to release the £4,000 I'd spent on the renovation of the property. But by renting the property I was able to make around 12% return per annum and was able to cover the entire monthly mortgage, insurance, maintenance and other costs and make some cash flow. It became clear that although the property was in negative equity, I could still make money from the monthly rental income. The only time the negative equity would affect me was if I had to sell, but in fact I still own the property now and its value in 2011 was around £180,000. This certainly drummed home the benefits of receiving a rental income whilst in the background my equity grows steadily. Although I am still of the belief that property should first and foremost give you cash flow, the added benefit of equity growth (the value of the property going up over time) is incredible.

I remember attending a property seminar sometime in the nineties when the presenter got us all to undertake a simple task of listing our assets and liabilities. He then proceeded to ask the people in the room what their greatest asset was. Apart from some non-homeowners, everyone listed their house as their largest asset. It ended up becoming quite competitive on whose house had grown most in value. Those who had owned their house for over 10 years were sitting in the seminar looking very proud of themselves as they had mostly doubled their

"I think the credit crunch is a brilliant thing. We should all stop moaning and start celebrating. When times are tough, it's an opportunity to start looking at life in a different way."

Jarvis Cocker

equity or even more. And then the presenter said something that has stuck with me ever since. He said, **'So why did you only buy one?'!!!** That one statement set me on my way to accumulating a property portfolio.

Until 2004 I had undertaken a combination of buy-to-let and buy-to-sell, but as property prices rose significantly, margins in buy-to-let were becoming much harder to achieve. Until this point I had been making a yield of around 12 to 15% per annum. In 2004, when everyone else started to pile into the buy-to-let boom, yields dropped significantly, because people were buying buy-to-let property with the strategy of just covering their costs, saying things like: 'as long as it wipes its face, it's okay'. That to me just meant no cash flow. At that point I decided to concentrate my efforts on developing property to sell, as property prices were increasing significantly. They were going up month on month. For the next four years, times were good; most of the projects I undertook were sold before the build was even finished and prices just kept going up.

That was until the credit crunch started. It was sometime in October 2007. I had just returned from holiday and I was totally out of touch with current affairs. You can imagine my surprise when I turned on the news channel to see people queuing outside the Northern Rock bank desperate to withdraw their money. Most people had seen the story evolve on the news from rumour to reality, whereas I was suddenly confronted with a run on a UK bank and rumours of other banks in trouble. Things like this didn't happen in a modern economy. It was just unheard of and unthinkable that scenes similar to the great depression were taking place on the streets outside a British bank. We have all found out the hard way that the banks are not the trustworthy solid institutions we thought they were.

By the time I'd realised we were in the Credit Crunch, developing property to sell became almost impossible, but fortunately for me, I was nearing the completion of our current development and only had three properties left to sell. By mid-

"The wisest rule in investment is: when others are selling, buy. When others are buying, sell. Usually, of course, we do the opposite. When everyone else is buying, we assume they know something we don't, so we buy. Then people start selling, panic sets in, and we sell too."

Jonathan Sacks

2008 I decided to rent these three remaining properties as not only had potential buyers disappeared but prices were also reducing significantly as the banks seemed to go into free fall and mortgages virtually dried up. It was at this point that the benefits of my rental portfolio really hit home. We all know how hard the economic climate has been during the recession – but thanks to a passive income created from my previous efforts investing in rental property, I didn't have to worry too much about the Credit Crunch.

There were a huge number of people who jumped on the buy-to-let bandwagon and a lot of those have had their fingers burnt simply because they had not really understood what they were doing. Most of them thought "How hard can it be? Just buy an investment property and chuck some tenants in it", but there's a bit more to it than that and if done properly your investment will grow to a situation where it pays you an income for life with very little effort required. What I have done is not get rich quick but get rich forever, and this takes effort, and depending on the effort that you're prepared to put in will determine how quickly you achieve financial freedom. This is not a race, it's an important life strategy. Some people will achieve freedom in a few short years, and others will take ten, possibly twenty years. This doesn't matter as long as you take control of your future and don't leave it to chance.

Someone recently said to me "It's all right for you; you got in to property at the right time". This isn't the case because any time is the right time. As long as you buy at the right price and you understand how the investment works and all the figures add up, any time can be the right time. For instance, I was investing in property back in 2007 when the market was at its peak and although the values of those properties have dropped, they still make me money. They still create cash flow. As I just said about the cottage I bought in 1991, the only time that the value would become a problem and I would make a loss, is if I had to sell. Remember what Warren Buffett said "Don't buy an investment you're not prepared to hold for at least 10 years".

"Risk comes from not knowing what you're doing."

Warren Buffet

I was fortunate in that I was able to learn from the last property downturn in the early 1990s. This led me to always ask the question, "What's the worst that can happen?" You see, if you don't know what the worst that could happen is, if it happens you won't be ready for it. This is why so many people lost their homes and businesses back in the recession of the early 1990s when interest rates rose dramatically. People couldn't meet their mortgage payments and loan repayments, which led to some of the highest levels of home repossession and bankruptcies we have ever experienced.

What caused the world recession that started around 2008? My personal view is that it was caused from greed by the banking industry. Apart from a few top analysts who were saying that the banks were overexposed and their business models were unsustainable, everyone else just made the most of the boom times including me. Even Gordon Brown the Chancellor of the Exchequer, who had run the UK economy for 10 years from 1997 was clueless; he had no idea what was about to happen. In June 2007 at the annual Mansion House Speech where he addressed the banking industry, he said, I quote: "History will record this as the beginning of a new golden age in banking". How wrong he was. Within three months of that speech, in September 2007, the Northern Rock building society ran out of money and had to be rescued by the UK government along with other banks such as Lloyds and Royal Bank of Scotland (RBS). Then not long after that, in 2008, the catalyst to the world recession happened when the American bank Lehman Bros collapsed. The problem had occurred due to banks being self-regulated. A group of top bankers would gather at Basel, Switzerland to set regulative standards for the banking industry. The problem with these regulations was that they were based on self-interest for the banks, and not based on the risk to their customers' money. They should have been working from the position 'What is the worst that could happen?' not, 'How can we make even more money?'

What can we do to stop this sort of thing happening again? Truthfully, not a lot. Unless someone can come up with a way

"As sure as the spring will follow the winter, prosperity and economic growth will follow recession."

Bo Bennett

of eliminating greed from the human race, these sort of things will always occur.

My own theory on recession is that it's a natural process in any economy. I like to equate it to the seasons. All economies go through ups and downs just like our seasons. We go from spring to summer in to autumn and finally into winter. Then we move back to spring and so it goes on. The only real difference is that our economies don't go through the seasons on an annual basis it's over a much longer period of time. If you think of an economy coming out of a period of recession (the recession obviously being winter). You start to see the young shoots of growth that would appear in spring. Then over a number of years we experience the good times with an economy yielding crops and bearing fruit again just like summer. Unfortunately, this is not sustainable. It is not possible to sustain high-growth and high yields for everyone all the time. Eventually things slow down and the leaves begin to fall, the economy moves into autumn and back into winter. The most important thing to learn from this is that it's a natural process, just like the seasons. The only people who fail are the ones who fail to provide adequately for the winter. In other words if you don't put some of your high yielding summer fruits aside to take you through the winter then you will be one of the casualties of recession. Now you know the natural flow and how an economy works you can be prepared for what each season provides.

I would say the best thing we could do is stop focusing on the doom and gloom that the media churn out on a daily basis, stop whingeing about the wider national economy and concentrate on what we can affect which is our own economy. Warren Buffet said, 'The best defence against a lagging economy is to create more income'. So remember to focus on your own economy, your own cash flow, your own expenditure - these are the things that if controlled properly will make you wealthy.

I firmly believe the most important thing about any investment is cash flow; your money must now make money. Don't choose

"Albert Einstein when asked what he considered to be the most powerful force in the universe answered: Compound interest! What you have become is the price you paid to get what you used to want."

Mignon McLaughlin

an investment that offers possible future growth; you don't want to be sitting around hoping for a return on your investment. You should be looking for at least an annual return on your money. You can then reinvest your returns so that it compounds and compounds. Albert Einstein once declared compound interest to be the most powerful force in the universe and was mans greatest discovery. You don't need to completely understand compounding. As I mentioned before if you just imagine each pound or dollar as an individual employee; as those employees set to work they create new employees and then those employees in turn create even more, until eventually you have a huge workforce all creating more and more. How big do you want your workforce to be?

To explain how powerful compounding can be, let me share this scenario with you. Imagine your parents started a Wealth Fund for you on the day you were born, and saved just £1 per day. This would create an initial Wealth Fund by your first birthday of £365, which they then invested and achieved 10% annual return. By continuing to save £1 per day, they would add another £365 every year to the original amount, and would also have compounding interest. By your 21st birthday, they would have created a Wealth Fund of over £23,000. If you then continued to do the same by adding £1 per day until you were 60 years old, just adding £365 per year to your fund and letting it compound, you would have a Wealth Fund of over £1million on your 60th birthday. I think you'll agree this may be a slightly better strategy than relying on the state pension, of next to nothing per week!

When you start investing your Wealth Fund, be cautious, don't take unnecessary risks. Understand your market, know at least the basics of your investment. Also try and invest in something that you enjoy, have a contingency plan, don't put all your money in one pot, spread your risk, seek out experts, carry proper insurance, and undertake thorough due diligence. This is all part of managing what you do and lowering the element of risk. Investing a lot of money in something you don't understand can be extremely risky. In Robert Kiyosaki's book 'Rich Dad Poor Dad', he says "There's a big difference between risk and risky". Of course there's always an element of risk in anything we do in life – but there's a difference between *risk* and *risky*... I aimed to understand and manage risk with a view to eliminating it completely. To give you a better understanding of what I mean when I'm talking about controlling risk – let me use a ladder as an analogy... The top of the ladder is success. The bottom of the ladder is where we all start out. Some people are so adverse to risk, they won't even step on the ladder. They stay on the ground safe and secure in the knowledge they can't fall... Some people race up the ladder to the top – and sometimes this works – but there's a high risk of falling... What I'm talking about is **managed risk** – where there are two people putting the ladder up, checking the ground is level, the angle is correct and the ladder is leaning on a secure surface... One person foots the ladder safely from the bottom and the other person climbs up and secures it at the top... This scenario takes longer and requires more effort **but** risk has been understood, managed and therefore controlled. This is the difference between *risk* and risky.

Why do I invest in property? I believe it's a simple and relatively straightforward investment. Saying that, property is quite a hands-on investment strategy and you will need to make sure you have the time to allocate to it without it affecting your day job. If you have a really busy career and you don't have a lot of spare time, you may want to look at hands-off investment strategies. There are plenty of other ways of making your money work hard for you. You just need to know where to look. If you're already an experienced investor, my ideas will help you improve your present investments and give you a solid plan on what you want to achieve in the future.

One of the reasons I talk about residential homes is that most of us already own or rent one, and although the process of buying a house may be stressful, it's not that difficult and I can virtually guarantee you don't have to give up your job to undertake the process, so if you can buy your home alongside the day job, you can buy an investment property too; it's virtually the same process - source a property, negotiate the price, organise a mortgage, get a survey, source a solicitor to complete the conveyancing and finally receive the keys to move in. Sorry, move some tenants in. It may have seemed stressful but in reality it's pretty straightforward, and I've met a number of people who overcomplicate it and just end up scaring people into thinking they can't do it. Although there is a process you need to follow and some things you need learn and get right, I can assure you it's all very simple because "If I can do it, you can too".

"Experience taught me a few things. One is to listen to your gut, no matter how good something sounds on paper. The second is that you're generally better off sticking with what you know. And the third is that sometimes your best investments are the ones you don't make."

Donald Trump

CHAPTER 10

My seven reasons

'd like to cover the reasons why I believe that property is still the simplest, most secure future-proof investment that there is, and if done properly will provide for you for the rest of your days, and create a legacy for your family, even after you're long gone. Now don't get me wrong, property isn't the only income-earning asset that you can acquire, but being that over 80% of the world's wealth is held in property, whether that's residential, commercial or land, it is simply one of the biggest commodities there is. It's the ground we stand on and we seem to value it above nearly anything else. Our desire for it has created more wars than even religion and we would do almost anything to protect it...

Here are my seven reasons why I invest in property and why I believe it's the best investment vehicle there is. I've just mentioned two of them so we might as well start there. The first reason is that it can be left to future generations, creating a legacy that could last for hundreds of years. They don't even need to know about property, it can be managed and they can benefit from the rental profits and the future growth in the value of the property. Much better than your average pension that dies with you. That's simple and pretty obvious.

Secondly, future proof. Property doesn't tend to change a great deal compared with other investments. A 100-year-old house

"It's tangible, it's solid, it's beautiful. It's artistic, from my standpoint, and I just love real estate."

Donald Trump

is perfectly adequate in today's market and as long as it's well maintained, it probably will be for another few hundred years. Also property doesn't tend to disappear, unlike businesses. In fact, when a property is demolished, the owner would usually receive payment for its value. This could be for various reasons, such as redevelopment. In some circumstances, a property will be knocked down due to the regeneration of an area. In this case the property owner would be paid its value. Another reason for property to meet its demise is by a tragedy such as fire, but any sensible property owner should have adequate insurance for this unfortunate situation. Whereas in business, if a company goes bankrupt, the owners, staff, creditors and any investors all lose. So all this makes property a very secure long-term investment.

Let me explain what I mean about future proof. If I were to offer you two scenarios, which one would you choose?

Scenario number one. You have a long-lost relative who has passed away and left you everything in their will. Fifty years ago, your relative was quite a successful person and had decided to invest their wealth in property. Your inheritance consists of five houses ranging from 50 to 100 years old with no mortgages on them; they have been maintained to a good standard and are all presently let to tenants. Their total value is about £500,000 with a rental income of £40,000 per year, which covers all the running costs and gives some good cash flow.

Scenario number two. This is the same as the first, apart from your relative decided to invest their wealth in buying shares. At first the shares did very well, in fact the shares made double the growth that property would have done, but then they made some bad investments and eventually lost a lot of value in the dot-com bubble when that burst. As for your inheritance, the share values today are about £120,000. Now I know in the second scenario they could have done much better by moving their investment and had more of a variety of stocks, but I'm just trying to make a point that business changes, especially

"A housing renaissance has begun. This may be hard to believe after the dizzying, six-year-long crash in home sales, construction and house prices. But housing turned the corner last year, and it will take off in 2013."

Mark Zandi

in the fast pace of business today, whereas property is a much steadier long-term investment. Therefore you don't have to worry too much about a property going out of fashion or being out of date and useless in a couple of years. It's because property is such a secure investment, that banks will lend you money against its value, using it as security, and this brings me to my next reason.

The third reason is probably my favourite, leverage or gearing. This is when you invest in property, and banks will lend money against your investment by way of a mortgage. This means that you can purchase more property than you have money for. Let me give you a comparison between property and the stock market. If you had £100,000 to invest in property, you could quite easily use it as a 25% deposit, obtain a 75% mortgage for £300,000 and purchase property to the value of £400,000 and again as long as you have undertaken the right due diligence, the rental return that your property generates will cover the monthly mortgage payments, other costs and give you some cash flow. The great thing about this is that as property prices go up, you will benefit from the rise in value of a £400,000 asset. In comparison to this, if we look at investing in the stock market, your £100,000 would be all you could invest as the bank would decline to lend you money against your investment simply because the stocks you are investing in don't offer the same security as property. In this very basic scenario, the money you invested in the stock market would have to perform at four times the return of your investment in property and this isn't taking into consideration the cash flow your rental income generates.

The fourth benefit to property investment is discount. If we go back to the stock market, the shares you purchase would have had a price and if you were to approach your broker and ask for a discount on the market price of the shares, he'd probably laugh out loud. Whereas with property, you don't have to offer the asking price, you can offer whatever you feel it's worth and the lower you can negotiate, the more profit you will

"I like thinking big. If you're going to be thinking anything, you might as well think big."

Donald Trump

make on your rental yield and long-term on the equity growth that the property achieves. This is probably one of the most important areas of property investing. Buying at the right price is fundamental to your success. In my experience, negotiating a good discount seals the success of a deal from the start when you purchase the property, rather than hoping for a good price when you sell.

The fifth benefit is demand. We will always need somewhere to live. In the past it wouldn't have been unusual to have a family of three generations living under one roof, but in today's society demand is growing. We have more divorces and people separating which suddenly means a family requires two homes. Also we are living longer and healthier which is good news for us but it increases the population. More people mean more homes, and there are other factors that drive the population up, such as immigration and birth rates. We are also becoming more affluent; the desire for a second home in the country or on the coast is becoming more and more popular as we try to escape from the cities and suburbia, all putting further strain on the housing market. As society grows, one of the biggest individual things creating demand is lack of supply. We're just not building enough new houses. If the government decided to make a concerted effort to resolve the housing shortage, it would take at least 20 to 30 years' work to catch up.

As things stand, it looks like housing demand is here to stay, and while there is demand, house prices will steadily grow, which is great news for property investors, but never forget what goes up must come down. Property is no different to any other market. Prices will go up and they will come down!!! But when you understand how to work out what's a good deal, and what's a bad deal, you will only buy properties that make financial sense. When you learn this, it doesn't matter what the market is doing. For example, as I mentioned earlier, back in 2004 when we were buying property to let, property prices in the UK had gone up significantly over the previous five years making it harder to find deals that would make the rental returns we were looking for. As

"If you go to work on your goals, your goals will go to work on you. If you go to work on your plan, your plan will go to work on you. Whatever good things we build end up building us."

Jim Rohn

property prices were rising, we decided to take advantage of the capital growth in property at the time and by 2005 approximately 80% of our business was developing property to sell and only 20% was to let; this was us simply understanding the market. And my point is, if you learn how something works and you do it properly, you can't fail to be successful.

The sixth benefit of property comes from some of my own experiences in business. I used to be the part owner of a retail chain of mobile phones stores, and we treated each individual shop as its own small profit centre and the more shops that we could open, the more profit we would make. I also treat each property that I own as an individual profit centre but that's where the similarity ends. You see, with my property, once it's rented and being looked after by a professional managing agent, there's not a lot I have to do. It becomes a self-operating business system. In comparison with my chain of retail shops, the workload was endless with staff, marketing, stock, administration and accounts - I could go on.

Compared with building a portfolio of rental properties part-time alongside my other business interests, there was an obvious advantage in being a property owner, versus a business operator. In my experience, starting a new business can be like stepping into the unknown as well as needing a huge commitment of time and money. Let's face it, there is no guarantee whether a new venture will prosper. It can take a good five years for a new business to bear fruit and another five to become established. Whereas, if you're buying property properly, it can be done part-time so you can carry on with the day job and it's relatively straightforward.

My seventh benefit of investing in property is that you can create extra value. Often a property will be sold below its market value due to it being run down and in need of renovation. There are lots of other ways of creating value, not just renovation. You can buy land and build from new, you can extend an existing property, change the use of a property, even split a larger building into

"If you want to go somewhere, it is best to find someone who has already been there."

Robert Kiyosaki

smaller units; there's lots of ways of creating extra value. I like the fact that you are more in control of your investment and you can work out all the costs and what the rental return or future sale value is likely to be prior to purchase and whether it's a worthwhile investment. Again, in comparison with an investment in the stock market, the only way your investment will grow and become worth more is by the shares going up in value. The problem with this is you have absolutely no say or influence in the profitability of the company (whose shares you have invested in). In effect, you are hoping and relying on other people to make the right decisions to make your future income. This seems to be a pretty risky strategy verging on gambling. Hopefully you're beginning to see why I prefer to invest in property.

Let's just quickly summarise those seven points:

1. Creating a legacy for future generations, much better than a pension that dies when you die.

2. Future proof. Property is a secure long-term investment.

3. Leverage. Property enables you to borrow money against your investment.

4. Discount. On your initial purchase, you can negotiate a discount giving you better value.

5. Demand will always go up. As our population expands, we will need more and more housing.

6. Each property becomes its own self sufficient profit centre.

7. Creating extra value by improving, extending or converting, you can make a property worth more than you paid for it.

The thing I love about property more than anything else is that I'm in control of my investment and not relying on other people's decisions. Although I wouldn't recommend you just go out and buy the first house you see, there's a lot to learn and you need to put together a well worked out strategy before you undertake any new venture, in whatever field it may be.

"An expert is someone who has succeeded in making decisions and judgements simpler through knowing what to pay attention to and what to ignore."

Edward de Bono

CHAPTER 11

Experts

Whatever you do with your Wealth Fund, one of the keys to creating wealth is using experts. You must have the best specialist knowledge in your chosen field. In this case, it applies to investing and creating a passive income. This is such a complex, diverse and dynamic area, it would take more than a lifetime to know everything about this subject. You will find certain elements that appeal and you enjoy doing which you can focus on because you'll do them well. However, just because you don't personally have specialist knowledge in the areas where you need it, it doesn't mean you can't gain access to that information. Other people specialise in these fields, and their knowledge can easily become your knowledge if they're on your team.

One of the most valuable lessons I learnt in business is finding a way to attract and reward people who brought far more experience and technical know-how than me in their field. None of us are an expert at everything. I could probably have muddled through myself, saving some money and achieving a mediocre job. I would also have made avoidable mistakes and taken a lot longer to get to the goal too.

In this same vein, if you want to start investing your Wealth Fund, would you look for an experienced investor from whom to glean information, or would you talk to your friend or family

"Strength does not come from winning. Your struggles develop your strengths. When you go through hardships and decide not to surrender, that is strength."

Arnold Schwarzenegger

member who has never invested in anything? I suspect you'll agree that you should look for an experienced investor.

However, many people will naturally seek advice from their friends or family. They're the people you trust and they probably won't charge you for the information so it's understandable. This can be the BIGGEST obstacle to your success. If you had a broken tooth and needed a filling, you would see a dentist, you wouldn't ask a plumber to help, would you? It seems a silly analogy, but really, some people will automatically go to those they know best for advice, even though those people have no relevant skills or experience. Whilst brainstorming with those closest to you can be a great idea, you MUST build a team of specialists around you, upon whom you can rely, and trust to give you the best information. It is imperative you seek out those knowledgeable in the areas you want information on, not those who just have a good opinion.

I never cease to be surprised by how many people offer me advice when I'm embarking on a new project of any type. These days I listen politely and screen the advice quickly but I mainly keep my brain free for information from those most qualified to give it. I've also found most of the negative comments and those most likely to throw me off course comes from the unqualified people. The positive and encouraging advice comes from the most knowledgeable and experienced experts and I listen and challenge my beliefs with the information they give me.

How can you tell if someone's an expert? This is easy; you simply ask them what they have achieved in the area of their particular expertise and as long as they can justify their claims of success, you can then decide on whether you want to work with them. This can be a little bit like interviewing someone for a job, so ask all the normal questions: What are your qualifications? What is your experience? How long have you been involved in this particular field of expertise? References and testimonials from previous clients? And maybe even a little bit about their background.

"Success is achieved by developing our strengths, not by eliminating our weaknesses."

Marilyn vos Savant

What are your weak points and strong points? Where do you need support, and which areas should you focus on? You may have been told at school that to improve in an area, you must work on your weaknesses. Whereas, the areas of a task, business or project in which I was strong were actually the ones I enjoyed most. The areas in which I was weak were the areas I least enjoyed. Therefore, I found it much easier to focus on my strengths than I did on my weaknesses, then used experts in the areas in which I was weak. We could all focus on our strengths and those things which we enjoyed the most. I don't need to tell you which approach was the most effective and enjoyable.

Knowing this, would you do what you learned at school, and work on your weaknesses, or would you **now** look at focusing on your strengths and find others to help out in your weak areas? Let's say you were setting up a new business to boost your income and you needed people to help you. Should you front the business and get someone else to do the accounting and back office tasks? This is definitely the most common train of thought and one which is appropriate for most people. However, if you are shy, and an accountant by trade, you may find it more fitting to employ sales people with you remaining in the background doing your accounts and ensuring that the company's finances are in great shape. If you are a natural front man or woman and accounts bore you to tears, then employing an accountant to look after your books would be sensible. The point I'm making is that you must cover every area suitably, and playing to your strengths and having others do the same on your behalf will increase productivity. Nowadays, when starting a new project I always map out the specialist areas I need covering and tick off the ones I am good at. Then of course I find the very best talent I can obtain for the level I need, and the budget I have. Or I find the budget to fit in with the talent I need. This also frees me up to focus on the things I am good at.

How does this theory affect your investing career? Well, you'll find an aspect or several aspects which really appeal to you, and about which you'll naturally want to become knowledgeable,

"An expert is someone who knows some of the worst mistakes, which can be made, in a very narrow field."

Niels Bohr

and the best you can be in this area. There will be other areas which need to be covered on your behalf, by people who are **years** ahead of you with knowledge and experience. Does that make you inferior to or less capable than them? Of course not. If you can use their knowledge, you have, in effect, achieved the same result as if you had spent years learning what they've learnt. Of course, most will need recompense for their knowledge, and much of the time, it holds true that you get what you pay for. However, if you're a new business with a small number of transactions, you certainly don't need the level of accountants, for example, that a major company will use. It's your job to know enough about the subject in question to assess the calibre of the person you're engaging, but you do not need to know the subject in detail, or indeed, know enough to carry out that particular function.

Take some time to work out what sort of things you enjoy and are good at. Is there a pattern? For example, if you are, or can learn to be good at, leading and organising a team, you'll do well at recruiting and managing the people you need to keep your money working well for you. These people may well change as your Wealth Fund and investments grow, as the level of knowledge and areas of expertise required will also change. Look at yourself as the Managing Director of your Wealth Fund, and imagine what specialists you'll need to help you move forward. You may have specialist knowledge already in a particular area and therefore you can fill that role. However, the point I'm making is that it would be a fallacy to think that you can cover all areas adequately in order to save money. This usually leads to a task becoming slow, laborious and tiresome and can often end up uncompleted due to loss of interest.

I am not solely responsible for the creation of my property portfolio. Over the years I've built up some great contacts who have been invaluable in their contribution. I have relationships with estate agents and property brokers who source property for me. I have built partnerships with mortgage brokers and

"Don't find fault, find a remedy; anybody can complain."

Henry Ford

banks that help me fund my projects, my solicitors who deal with the conveyancing and all the other legal aspects of my business. My architect is an invaluable member of my expert team dealing with the constant changes in planning and building regulations. I have a great firm of accountants who not only organise my accounts, but bring invaluable advice on business development. I also have great relationships with letting agents, tradesmen such as builders, plumbers, electricians, gardeners, window cleaners, to name but a few.

The point is I don't need to know all about these things. I just have to build relationships with reliable people whom I can trust and use their expertise to help create my success. Using experts and other people's knowledge is one of the most effective business strategies to use for success. Yet it is probably one of the least used. People seem to think that they are saving money by doing everything themselves. Whereas using a professional will often give you a better and quicker result and leave you free to concentrate on the things you enjoy and that you're an expert at. It's a simple choice between being a jack of all trades yourself and achieving a faster, quality job by using others. Take this book for instance, although I wrote the main body of text myself you will have noticed by now I have been able to draw on a huge amount of knowledge from other people by using their quotes to make my message a lot more powerful and profound. As well as things like the design of the book cover, editing my often unreadable text, print and production, creation of my website, marketing and distribution. I haven't done all these things myself I have sought out experts in each of these areas.

To make my point about using experts, I'm going to share a true story about Henry Ford, the founder of the Ford Motor Company. People said he was mad to think every home should have a car and that they shouldn't just be something for the rich and wealthy. In his striving to create an affordable car for the masses, he invented the first production line, now widely used throughout manufacturing. Although he was very successful, there were a group of academics who accused him of being stupid and challenged him to a test,

"If you don't design your own life plan, chances are you'll fall into someone else's plan."

Jim Rohn

(So good... I've used this quote twice.)

to which he happily accepted. An appointment was made for the academics to come up with a list of questions and they would meet Mr Ford at his offices to pose these. At the meeting, the first question was asked. Mr Ford listened intently and then turned to a panel on his desk where he typed in some numbers. Soon a voice replied, 'Yes Mr Ford, how can I help?' Mr Ford repeated the question and asked for the answer as soon as possible.

The academics were outraged. They accused him of cheating and said that their point was proven - he was stupid. Mr Ford sat calmly and said, 'Ask me another question.' So they returned to the list and asked the second question. Mr Ford again turned to the panel and typed in a number. This time it was a lady's voice. 'Yes Mr Ford, how can I help?' 'Could you come in here with a pen and paper please?' he replied. When she arrived, Mr Ford asked her to calculate the answer to the question. She sat on a table across the office and started to work out the answer. Again, the academics accused Mr Ford of cheating. At this point there was a knock on the door and in walked the gentleman who had been asked the first question. He said, "Excuse me, Mr Ford. I have the answer to the question that you required," and handed him a piece of paper. Then the woman stood up from the desk and walked across the room and handed him another piece of paper. Once the academics calmed down and stopped accusing him of cheating, Mr Ford looked at them and said 'I don't need to know all the answers, I just need to know the people with all the answers'. The academics asking the questions never achieved anything more than mediocrity, whereas Henry Ford went on to be one of the greatest entrepreneurs of the last century.

As I said, during our education and working life we are told to try harder and put more effort in to the areas we're weakest in. Instead, we would be better working hard and perfecting the things we are good at and enjoy, whilst employing experts and other people's knowledge to undertake the tasks we're not as good at.

Ok! Onto the final part of this book, putting into action everything that we have talked about. Creating your secure financial future.

"Nothing can stop the man with the right mental attitude from achieving his goal; nothing on earth can help the man with the wrong mental attitude."

Thomas Jefferson

CHAPTER 12

Life plan

This is the most important element in this book, as it brings together all the individual parts of what we've covered as a focused plan of action. It's simply not enough to just understand how and why these principles of wealth creation work. The whole focus on what you have taken on board must now be put into action. *Knowledge is useless if it is not acted upon.* A lot of what we will cover in this section will be going back over the things you've learnt and using them to create your personal life plan. Why is a plan so important? It turns your hopes and wishes into a targeted list of actions and more importantly it focuses you on the tasks you need to undertake.

This plan will start with what you really want out of life. As this is normally a big desire, it will provide the motivation you need to undertake the tasks you must complete in order for you to reach your goal. The rest of the plan will be the building blocks to get you to these goals. Before you start building your life plan, it's important that we recap some of the points we mentioned earlier in the book. Your goals and desires that you set out to achieve need to be real burning desires. You must be really passionate about what you want to achieve and for this reason it needs some serious time, thought and discussion. This is so serious, I would suggest you take a weekend or a couple of days out of your normal busy life and totally focus on what it is you want in life.

"Don't let the fear of the time it will take to accomplish something stand in the way of your doing it. The time will pass anyway; we might just as well put that passing time to the best possible use."

Earl Nightingale

How passionate do you need to be about your future? Well, this is a little bit extreme but I think it makes the point. It's about someone who has just been told by their doctor they have a very rare condition, leaving them only a couple of years to live. The good news was that a 100% effective cure existed, but it costs £1 million. Put any of us in that position and I'll guarantee every one of us would raise £1 million in a couple of years. Therefore, get passionate about your focus in life. The main thing we cover in the book is replacing your earned income with passive income, being free from having to work for money. Now surely that's something we can all get passionate about! But then what would you do with your time?

I want to really drive home the message about time, as I think it's an area that gets overlooked when we start thinking about things like fast cars, boats and luxury holidays. Don't forget it's the time you have doing the things you want, with the people you love, that really counts. How you feel is so much more important than any material possessions you have, therefore you should want to be wealthy to free up your time. I think it's worth reminding you of the time and money chart that was also covered earlier in the book. Knowing what category you are in is an important part of working out your present financial position.

1.   You have a small amount of time available and little money.

2.   You have lots of time available but very little money.

3.   You have very little time but lots of money.

4.   You have lots of time and lots of money.

"Take up one idea. Make that one idea your life - think of it, dream of it, live on that idea. Let the brain, muscles, nerves, every part of your body, be full of that idea, and just leave every other idea alone. This is the way to success."

Swami Vivekananda

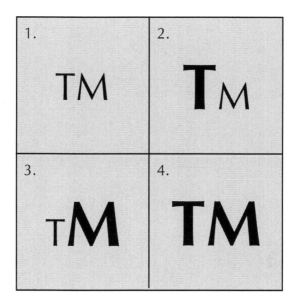

Obviously, the fourth category of having lots of time and money would be an ideal situation and having a focus on becoming time and money free should form an important part of your plan.

Remember the story about the magic bank account? You have 1,440 minutes in every day, so invest them wisely. Money can be made, spent and made again but time can only be spent, so make the most of it...

Most people's definition of wealth is having lots of money. The fact is money itself doesn't make us happy but it enables us not to have to work giving us the time and freedom to enjoy life. Hopefully you now understand that the true definition of wealth is having enough passive unearned income so that you can afford your lifestyle and more importantly free up your time so that you can enjoy it.

Your long-term goals must create passion and drive. This becomes your WHY! Remember the WHAT Formula, you can use this as a basis to build your plan.

"You were born to win, but to be a winner, you must plan to win, prepare to win, and expect to win."

Zig Ziglar

(W + H) x A = T

Reason **WHY** + Method **HOW** x **ACTION** = **TIME** Freedom

Success comes from doing something well, and to do something well we first need a good reason WHY to do it, then to accomplish whatever it is you want to undertake, we need a well worked-out method i.e. HOW. Having a good reason 'WHY' and a method 'HOW' will motivate us to take ACTION. Finally, the success we achieve from our actions will lead to TIME and freedom from having to work for money. This will form a framework for your plan. Your plan will be a route-map of the steps you need to achieve to get from where you are now, to your long-term goals.

For your plan to work effectively, you must totally believe in it. Rid yourself of any negativity; it's so important to understand that if your present thoughts and beliefs are negative, you will get negative results, so you must work on changing your thoughts and habits.

Having read and understood this book, your thoughts about money should be a lot more positive. Remember, money is simply a tool and it doesn't matter whether you're well off or broke – like any tool, you need to know how to use it. Once you know how to use money properly, it just gets easier and easier, and by implementing your plan you will automatically learn how to make money, make money.

So now your thoughts and beliefs about money have changed, you should genuinely believe that you can become wealthy. For some of us, this will still be hard to believe but once you start work on your plan, the feeling of achievement will drive you to want more success and it's true what they say, 'success breeds success'. Our focus now is to create new beliefs and habits on how you think and deal with money. Don't forget you need to believe that money is merely a tool, that it's easy to control and that it's simple to create.

"You will become as small as your controlling desire; as great as you dominant aspiration."

James Allen

Part of your plan will be about using your Wealth Fund to create a passive income. It will be your choice how you do this. You must work out what suits you and your lifestyle. Putting your Wealth Fund to work for you is a key part of your plan and can be implemented by some learning on your part. But remember this isn't a journey you need to undertake on your own as part of your plan will be seeking out and using experts.

Let's just recap on why we focus on building a passive income. As you now know, the way we measure wealth is by working out how long you could survive financially if your 'earned income' stopped. Remember we went through a scenario where you needed £5,000 a month to maintain your present lifestyle. If you had to stop work and you had £10,000 of savings, you could only cover two months of your living costs. In this case your wealth would last two months. To be financially free, you need to create a passive income of £5,000 per month for the rest of your life. This could be achievable for many of us over the next 10 years. I know we keep coming back to it but it won't happen without an effective plan in place.

Now, don't worry about what investments you're going to have to make to create your passive income, this comes later. Remember, follow the steps in the order that they are laid out. Then, when you've built your Wealth Fund, opportunities will present themselves because this is what you'll be focused on. Remember the Law of Attraction, 'what you think about will come about'.

Now let's have a look at how we're actually going to build our plan. Visually, it is like a route planner for a journey and the most important thing about any journey is knowing the destination. So, by using a journey as an analogy, the destination of your plan will be your long term goal. When you know the destination, you can plan a route from your current position or starting point. In planning this journey, we work it backwards starting at the destination. In other words, we're going to start off looking at your long-term goals and then look at what milestones need to be met in order to get you there.

"What you get by achieving your goals is not as important as what you become by achieving your goals."

Henry David Thoreau

Long-Term Focus

When you create your plan, your long-term focus should be built around having enough passive income to support your ideal lifestyle, not just your current lifestyle. Just imagine getting up each day and being able to do whatever you desire. Is it the material things in life that motivate you, such as cars, a bigger house and luxury holidays? Try the exercise we mentioned earlier in the book that helps you work out what material things you would like in your life. Remember the scenario of winning the lottery. Yes, I know from what you've learnt in the book you should invest a large portion of this so that it can go to work for you, but just for this exercise, let your mind run riot on what you would buy on a million pound/dollar shopping spree, as this should help you create your long-term focus.

Maybe your focus is being able to send your children to the right school or university, eating out in top restaurants, having more time at home with your family, working for yourself, deciding what parts of the world you would like to see, having less stress and more freedom. Is your motivation built around security? What would happen to your family if you fell ill and couldn't work anymore? What provisions have you made for your retirement? Do you have a pension? What will it be worth? Is your mortgage paid off? What do you really want to do in your lifetime? Do you want to make a difference to a favourite charity? How about leaving a legacy for future generations? Are you interested in what people will say about you when you've gone?

This will be very personal as we all have different desires. If you have a partner or spouse, it's obviously worth working together so you can help each other achieve your goals. As I've already mentioned, it's the things you really desire most that will give you true direction and purpose, so put some quality time aside and some serious thought into what you truly want out of life. This can often be one of the hardest things to work out but it is crucial that you do because without direction you are drifting around going nowhere through life. Do you remember the comparison between

*"Action is the foundational
key to all success."*

Pablo Picasso

a ship with an experienced crew and a piece of driftwood? The ship will get to its destination because it has a well charted route and a reason for getting there, whereas driftwood will just bob about and end up wherever the tide takes it.

Brainstorming

The best way to approach this is to simply brainstorm loads of ideas. Just write down anything that comes into your head that you might like to incorporate into your life. Don't worry about what order they're in or whether you think they are even possible - just write them all down. Once you have written down all your ideas, categorise each item in order of importance. Category 1 is the most important to you and category 3 is least important – something you would like, but it's certainly not as desirable to you as an item in Category 1.

Here is an example.

Brainstorm ideas for your long term goals	Category 1-2-3
Own an Aston Martin	3
Start my own charity	1
Pay off my mortgage	2
Pay for my children to go to private school	1
Five-star luxury holidays	2
Build my own dream home	1

Now that you've written down and categorised your ideas, it should be easy to define your long-term goals. Remember, these will give you the direction and purpose that will become the foundation of your plan. You now need to write a 'Personal Statement' so that you can visualise how you would like your life to be. This will be based on the high-category ideas you had. Your statement should be at least a couple of concise

"A real decision is measured by the fact that you've taken a new action. If there's no action, you haven't truly decided."

Tony Robbins

paragraphs but can be as long as you want. It should show a clear vision of your future and what you would like to be, do, have and how this future would make you feel. I would also highly recommend you create a vision board of pictures and images of all the things that you want in your life.

From Goals to a Plan of Action

Goals are important – they are what we create our Plan of Action from – and your Plan of Action will be the tasks you need to carry out on a daily basis to achieve your dreams and goals. Simple! Now that you have your long-term objectives and mission laid out, it's time to form some intermediate goals and targets to help keep you on track. Whatever your mission, it's highly likely that you'll need time and income to achieve your long-term goals, therefore it makes sense to build your intermediate goals around creating a passive income.

For the purposes of this plan, we are going to concentrate on the elements you've learnt about in this book and set a main focus on matching your present income with a passive income. Most of this plan will be focused around your finances, career and income. The short-term and perhaps medium-term objectives (depending on your circumstances) of this plan are to create a Wealth Fund that will be put to work to build your passive income. Your dreams and goals in your mission will provide the passion and desire that will motivate you to undertake the tasks required to achieve your dreams.

Our long-term goals can often seem overwhelming and unachievable, so as we covered in the book earlier, we now need to cut them down to size by concentrating on our short-term goals over the first three years. These should be about improving your cash flow by taking control of your monthly expenditure and creating more income, allocating your money using the 80-20 rule, getting out of debt, creating a Wealth Fund, and a Contingency Fund then eventually investing for a passive income.

Below is an example of how a three-year goal is broken down to give you the tasks required in your first week. So by starting with a target in three years, you can see how we break down the first three years into individual years. Then year one is a plan of action targeted at specific tasks by splitting year one into quarters, with the first quarter being split into three individual months. The first month is split in to four separate weeks and your focus can be the work required in the first week by using a weekly planner. This way, you end up with a daily task list for every day until you reach your long-term goals but you only have to plan the milestones and the tasks required for each day. It's actually very simple - just set yourself easy-to-achieve tasks and keep achieving!

This example is very brief and is just to show how a three year goal can be broken down to the tasks required in week one.

3 Year Plan - Example

Three Year Goal

- Save £25k deposit to purchase my first buy-to-let investment property

- Start talking to estate agents about looking for an investment property

- Complete a 100 mile bike ride in one day to raise money for charity

Two year goal

(What I need to achieve in two years to be on target for my three year goal)

- Save £15k towards deposit on a buy-to-let investment property

- Enter a 100km time trial bike ride

One year goal

(What I need to achieved in year one to be on target for my two year goal)

- Save £5k towards deposit on a buy-to-let investment property

- Start training twice a week on my bike

Month nine target

(What I need to achieved to be on target for my one year goal)

- Save £2,500 towards deposit on a buy-to-let investment property

- Attend a course on buy to let property

Month six target

(What I need to achieved to be on target for my nine month target)

- Pay off £5k debt (go out and celebrate)

- Start saving for deposit on a buy to let investment property

- Join my local landlord association

Month three target

(What I need to achieved to be on target for my 6 month target)

- Pay off £2,500 debt

- Research property courses and seminars

- Purchase a new bike

- Start networking with like-minded people at property events

Week four target

(What I need to achieve to be on target for my three month target)

- Complete restructuring of monthly income/expenditure to within the 80/20 rule

- Pay off £835 from debt

- Subscribe to buy-to-let industry magazines and blogs

- Change utility suppliers

- Start walking to work twice a week

Week three target

(What I need to achieve to be on target for my four week target)

- Start part-time job to supplement income

- Research and learn about the buy-to-let market

- Attend weekly keep-fit class

- Plan to save on household bills

Week two target

(What I need to achieve to be on target for my three week target)

- Allocate 20% of income to reduce debt

- Scrutinise credit card and bank statements and stop unnecessary payments

- Start looking for secondary income

- Change diet to eat more healthy food

Week one target

(What I need to achieve to be on target for my two week target)

- Complete my first weekly planner

- Work out my present cash flow using the income and expenditure chart

- Work out debt repayment plan

- Look at ways to keep fit and healthy

Now simply use the weekly planner provided and keep achieving your daily tasks!!!!!!

To tie all this together, the route map from where you are now, to your long-term focus is already in place – just follow these steps but before you do you must have created your long-term goals and lifestyle plan.

STEP 1
Long-term goals
create a vision of the lifestyle
you would like to live

STEP 2
Understand your present
cash flow position by working
out your budget

STEP 3
Create a new financial lifestyle
using the 80-20 rule

STEP 4
Be GOOD
(Get Out Of Debt)

STEP 5
Build Capital and create a
Wealth Fund

STEP 6
Protect your wealth against
unforeseen circumstances by creating a
Contingency Fund

STEP 7
Investment for a passive income
using experts and other
people's knowledge

SUMMARY

1. The First step is to create a long-term focus. This must give you passion and drive for your future life.

2. The Second step is to understand your financial position by using the income and expenditure list. It's crucial that you know where your present cash flow stands. This is the difference between your total monthly income and your total monthly expenditure. You must enter all of your income and expenditure items, however small or insignificant they may seem. Even small everyday costs like grabbing a coffee on the way to work or downloading an app for your phone. It's often these small stealth payments that you don't even notice that can create a significant saving on your expenditure.

3. The Third step is to organise your financial lifestyle to run within the 80:20 rule – a maximum of 80% of your income is used for your lifestyle, leaving 20% to pay off debts or build a Wealth Fund. To do this, you may need to increase your income. This will shorten the length of time it takes you to achieve your goals and is a much more positive approach to wealth creation than cutbacks and austerity measures.

4. The Fourth step is to get rid of bad debt, if you have any. The course that we have created that complements this book goes into a lot more detail and has specialist software

including a debt reduction programme to help you reduce your debt in the most cost-effective way. It also has a budgeting program specifically designed to help you work your finances within the 80-20 rule, and lots more.

5. The Fifth step is to build your Wealth Fund, ready for investing.

6. The Sixth step is to put in place an effective Contingency Fund to suit your circumstances.

7. The Seventh and final step is to invest your Wealth Fund for a passive income which will help take you to your long-term focus/goal.

Where these steps actually fit in with your short-term, medium-term and long-term goals will depend on your circumstances, such as level of debt, income and desire to learn and take action. Therefore, it would be wrong of me to partition these steps into specific time frames for you but you must plan them out with time frames.

Finally, before we get to actually creating this plan, it's important to understand that when you write down your ambitions or goals, they must be believable, specific, time focused and have a clear method.

Believable:

If you focus on something you don't really believe that you can achieve, you will end up using excuses such as "I knew that was impossible."

Specific:

The more detail you write down, the more real something becomes. For instance, it's no good just saying, "I want a new car" – be more specific about what make, model, colour and what features and extras it has. The more detail, the better as we need to know that we have reached and achieved our goals. By being specific, you can't cheat yourself with a cheap bottom of the range car when your actual goal was a top of the range model! This is where a vision board can help you focus.

Time Focused:

Without a planned achievement date on your goals, there's no sense of urgency. Each goal must have a date by which you want to achieve it. Without a date, your goal is merely wishful thinking!

Method:

Do you know how to achieve your goal? It doesn't matter if you don't have a method right now and it certainly shouldn't stop you from making a goal, but you will need to work this out in due course. Which experts might you need help and advice from to achieve your goal? Do you require further knowledge and learning?

On the following pages you'll find specific sheets to help you with your plan. (Extra sheets Free from **www.therichrevolution.com**)

The question I'm asked most frequently is... 'What should I invest in?' First you need to create your wealth fund. As for investing this is your choice but by visiting the website **www.therichrevolution.com** and subscribing to my blog I will share lots of great ideas on wealth creation and investing. But for now focus on your plan. Also on the website find out about the step-by-step program that takes you from where you are now, to fulfilling your plan. This includes some amazing software for budgeting, debt reduction and a special program to calculate how your investments will compound and grow.

To:

Remember this is your plan so fill it out how it best serves you. I would recommend you make an appointment with yourself once a week to review your plan and read your personal statement. Then use the weekly planner to set out the tasks required that week, then break these down into daily to do lists, this should become a habit, you should be sitting down once a day and ticking off the things that you've achieved and writing a new list for the next day. Don't forget your plan must be focused but also flexible to fit in with your life. The secret is to do this every day with out fail and never give up.

So we've now reached the end of the book, this leaves you two choices. You can either choose to carry on with your life the way it is. Or you can choose to follow a path that creates wealth!!! – YOU WILL FEEL HEALTHIER, FULL OF LIFE, AND EXPERIENCE A CALM SENSE OF STABILITY, just by taking action.

Let me ask you this. If you were to go back three years how was your life financially? Since then have things changed significantly? Have you achieved your goals? Do you have all the things you want in life? Let me ask you something else. Having compared your financial life three years ago with how it is today, if you carry on doing what you're doing, what do you think your life will be like three years from now??? One more question. What do you think your life could be like if you changed paths and worked with us on creating a plan for your financial freedom??? To find out more visit **www.therichrevolution.com**

My wish for you is that you create a clear focused plan for your future and remember. "It's not what you earn, it's what you do with what you earn"!!!

I'd like to finish with one final quote that a good friend wrote in my 40th birthday card.

'Live long, laugh lots, love life'.

Join the RICH REVOLUTION at **www.therichrevolution.com**

WORK SHEETS

Step 1

Long-term goals to create a vision of the lifestyle you would like to live. Remember, to help you with this, imagine you've just won the lottery, so some of the things you think of may feel or seem totally unrealistic but write them down anyway.

Brainstorm ideas for your long-term goals	Categorise 1-2-3

Using the ideas from the brainstorming exercise above, create a personal statement of how you would like your life to be in 10 years' time.

My life 10 years from now:

....

....

....

....

....

....

Step 2

Understand your present cash flow position by working out your budget.

This list will help you work out your income and expenditure. The focus here is to have 20% more income than your expenditure, and this can then be used to pay off any bad debt and if you have no bad debt then it can be saved to create your Wealth Fund.

Monthly Income	Amount	Monthly Expenditure	Amount
Main Income		Mortgage/rent	
Second Income		Bank loan	
Investment Income		Personal loans	
Interest on Savings		Consolidation loan	
Family Allowance		Home improvement loan	
Disabled/Other Benefits		Credit card	
Pension Payments		Store card	
Child Maintenance		Car loan	
Part-time Income		Overdraft	
		Bank interest	
		Bank charges	
		Payday loans	
		Catalogue payment	
		Council tax	
		Electricity bill	
		Gas bill	
		Water	
		Phone bill	
		Mobile phone	

		Internet/broadband	
		TV licence	
		Satellite TV subscription	
		Magazine subscription	
		Memberships	
		Self-employed tax contribution	
		Car maintenance	
		Car tax	
		Car finance	
		Car insurance	
		Car fuel	
		Travel	
		Buildings insurance	
		Contents insurance	
		Life insurance	
		Critical illness insurance	
		Sickness and accident insurance	
		Pet insurance	
		Groceries	
		Clothing	
		Household maintenance	
		Gardener	
		Window cleaner	
		Cleaner	
		School dinners	
		School fees	
		Child maintenance	

		Pocket money	
		Entertainment	
		Holidays	
		Hobbies	
		Christmas fund	
		Eating out	
		Lottery/betting	
		Cigarettes/alcohol	
		Snacks/treats	
		Lunches	
		Other daily expenses	
Total Income		**Total Expenditure**	
Total cash flow		**(income minus expenditure)**	

Step 3

Create a new financial lifestyle using the 80-20 rule. 80% of your income should cover your lifestyle and living costs and 20% is put towards creating a Wealth Fund.

Make a list of tasks required to achieve this. You may need to make some cutbacks on your present expenditure, creating some extra income or maybe a bit of both.

List of tasks

....

....

....

....

....

....

....

....

....

....

....

....

....

....

....

Step 4

Be GOOD (Get Out Of Debt). This can sometimes be a very complex issue and you may need to use an expert to help you. If you're fortunate enough to not have any bad debt then move straight on to the next step.

List of tasks

....

....

....

....

....

....

....

....

....

....

....

....

....

....

....

....

....

Step 5

Build Capital and create a Wealth Fund. Initially your funds will be relatively small so while they build, it would be best to keep them in the highest interest-earning account you can find.

List of tasks

....

....

....

....

....

....

....

....

....

....

....

....

....

....

....

....

....

....

Step 6

Protect your wealth against unforeseen circumstances by creating a Contingency Fund.

I personally don't have a Contingency Fund. Instead I have an emergency credit card and if I need to use it I then focus on clearing it as soon as I can. I prefer that all my available funds are working for me at all times. You will have to make your own decisions on the strategy you create.

List of tasks

....

....

....

....

....

....

....

....

....

....

....

....

....

....

Step 7

Invest for a passive income using experts and other people's knowledge.

This is the most complex part of your Life Plan. I would suggest that some of your first tasks are to start researching different types of investment ideas and what sorts of returns you can make. This is a good exercise, as once you have built your Wealth Fund you will already understand the investments you want to make and be knowledgeable about how you want to put your money to work.

List of tasks

....

....

....

....

....

....

....

....

....

....

....

....

....

....

3 Year Plan

Three Year Goal

....

....

....

....

....

Two Year Goal

(What I need to achieve in two years to be on target for my three year goal)

....

....

....

....

....

One Year Goal

(What I need to achieve in year one to be on target for my two year goal)

....

....

....

....

....

Month Nine Target

(What I need to achieve to be on target for my one year goal)

....

....

....

....

Month Six Target

(What I need to achieve to be on target for my nine month target)

....

....

....

....

Month Three Target

(What I need to achieve to be on target for my six month target)

....

....

....

....

Week Four Target

(What I need to achieve to be on target for my three month target)

....

....

....

....

Week Three Target

(What I need to achieve to be on target for my four week target)

....

....

....

....

Week Two Target

(What I need to achieve to be on target for my three week target)

....

....

....

....

Week One Target

(What I need to achieve to be on target for my two week target)

....

....

....

....

Now simply use the weekly planner to list out the tasks you need to achieve.

Then, just keep achieving.

Weekly Planner

Week commencing: ....

Objectives for this week

....

....

....

....

....

....

....

....

....

....

Actions required

....

....

....

....

....

....

....

....

....

....

Daily task list

Monday:

....

....

....

....

Tuesday:

....

....

....

....

Wednesday:

....

....

....

....

Thursday:

....

....

....

....

Friday:

....

....

....

....

Weekly Planner

Week commencing: ....

Objectives for this week

....

....

....

....

....

....

....

....

....

....

Actions required

....

....

....

....

....

....

....

....

....

....

Daily task list

Monday:

....

....

....

....

Tuesday:

....

....

....

....

Wednesday:

....

....

....

....

Thursday:

....

....

....

....

Friday:

....

....

....

....

Weekly Planner

Week commencing: ....

Objectives for this week

....

....

....

....

....

....

....

....

....

....

Actions required

....

....

....

....

....

....

....

....

....

....

Daily task list

Monday:

....

....

....

....

Tuesday:

....

....

....

....

Wednesday:

....

....

....

....

Thursday:

....

....

....

....

Friday:

....

....

....

....

Weekly Planner

Week commencing: ....

Objectives for this week

....

....

....

....

....

....

....

....

....

....

Actions required

....

....

....

....

....

....

....

....

....

....

Daily task list

Monday:

....

....

....

....

Tuesday:

....

....

....

....

Wednesday:

....

....

....

....

Thursday:

....

....

....

....

Friday:

....

....

....

....

Weekly Planner

Week commencing: ....

Objectives for this week

....

....

....

....

....

....

....

....

....

....

....

Actions required

....

....

....

....

....

....

....

....

....

....

....

Daily task list

Monday:

....

....

....

....

Tuesday:

....

....

....

....

Wednesday:

....

....

....

....

Thursday:

....

....

....

....

Friday:

....

....

....

....

Weekly Planner

Week commencing: ....

Objectives for this week

....

....

....

....

....

....

....

....

....

....

Actions required

....

....

....

....

....

....

....

....

....

....

....

Daily task list

Monday:

....

....

....

....

Tuesday:

....

....

....

....

Wednesday:

....

....

....

....

Thursday:

....

....

....

....

Friday:

....

....

....

....

*"Work your way
out of work by
accumulating assets."*

Bruce Bishop

ABOUT THE AUTHOR

How many entrepreneurs and business experts do you know who have dyslexia? Richard Branson, Alan Sugar, Steve Jobs… well it's time to add another name to the list! Bruce Bishop, the founder of The Rich Revolution. His mission is to empower people through independent financial freedom.

He began his working life as a labourer in the building industry having left school with a handful of very mediocre qualifications, due to his struggle with dyslexia.

In his early twenties when most people his age were listening to their favourite music on the radio, Bruce was listening to self-development and motivational audio books, which inspired him to start his own business.

During his working life Bruce owned various businesses and had set out with the ambition and focus to create a company of great value, so he could exit for millions and retire in the lap of luxury.

Things didn't quite work out as planned. In fact Bruce never made more than a reasonable income from the businesses he owned, the thing that really made his wealth is what he did with that income…

In his early thirties he made a plan to re-invest a proportion of his earnings to create a passive income. It was this strategy that enabled him to retire from business at the age of 44. He only wishes that he had been taught these strategies earlier in life, as they can be applied to any form of asset or investment and it doesn't matter whether you're in debt or wealthy, the strategies work for everyone!

Bruce is often heard saying: It's not WHAT you earn, it's what you DO with what you earn.

Bruce's mission is to truly help others to become financially independent and regain control of their lifestyle. He believes wealth is not just about having financial security but also, more importantly, the time and freedom it gives you to spend with those that you love.

By revealing the powerful strategies in his book 'THE RICH REVOLUTION' people develop an understanding of the simple laws of money and apply them through a custom formulated plan to create a Wealth Fund.

If people want to grow their accumulated Wealth Fund quicker they are invited to attend seminars to support them in creating a Rich Revolution Life Plan and they also gain access to a trusted Investment Network for people to discover opportunities to invest in.

Bruce is convinced that the world will hit another financial crisis with pensions and retirement plans not creating much worth and nations having to support people through social benefits. It's time to give 'People back the Power through financial independence'.

Take responsibility for your wealth today and join The Rich Revolution!

www.therichrevolution.com

Printed in Great Britain
by Amazon.co.uk, Ltd.,
Marston Gate.